Are You Ready for School?

Are You Ready for School?

Trust, Collaboration and Enquiry Between Parents and Teachers

Andrew Oberthur

Copyright © Andrew Oberthur 2021

All rights reserved. No part of this book may be reproduced or transmitted in any form or by any means, electronic or mechanical, including photocopying, recording or by any information storage and retrieval system, without prior permission in writing from the publisher.

First published as *Are You Ready for Primary School This Year?* in 2008 by Peak Performance Development.
This revised and updated edition is published by Amba Press in 2021.

Amba Press
Melbourne, Australia
www.ambapress.com.au

Editor—Francesca Hoban Ryan
Cover Designer—Alissa Dinallo
Illustrations—Gail Semiao of scribbleline

Printed by IngramSpark

ISBN: 9781922607126 (pbk)
ISBN: 9781922607133 (ebk)

A catalogue record for this book is available from the National Library of Australia.

PRAISE FOR *ARE YOU READY FOR SCHOOL?*

I think the trio of key concepts—trust-collaboration-enquiry—is dynamite. I found this very helpful for any relationship.

Steve Biddulph, psychologist and
author of Raising Boys and Raising Girls

A strong resource for parents and teachers! I'll certainly be recommending it on my school travels.

Madonna King, journalist and author of Ten-Ager

The book clearly demonstrates a wealth of experience and knowledge built up over many years from someone at the coalface. Most parent-school tensions could be avoided if the chapter on diplomatic questions at school—which explains how to handle difficult queries and situations—was read by all parents and teachers.

Blaise Joseph, Research Fellow at the Centre
for Independent Studies in Sydney

This book covers essential elements of the teacher / parent relationship. It contains sound advice and strong examples of the types of issues that arise on a day-to-day-basis in schools. These are the issues that matter to parents.

Clive Dixon, freelance educator,
former Regional Director for Department of Education,
Training and Employment (Queensland)

How do we prepare our children for the various transitions they will encounter? Getting ready for prep? Between years? Entering a new school? Andrew Oberthur has nailed it! Every page has gems, every chapter provides a detailed roadmap of the path you / we all need to transverse.

Allan Parker OAM, micro-
behavioural scientist and negotiator

A must-read for parents as they are their children's first teachers.

Dr Kevin Donnelly AM, Senior Research Fellow at Australian Catholic University

Andrew navigates the ever-evolving school context with a sensibility and knowledge that can be understood by teachers and parents alike. A practical mix of tips, tricks and observations filtered through a modern lens for the modern parent / teacher. A must-read!

James Edwards, early-career teacher

At times it can be difficult to know how to approach challenging or difficult situations that arise within schools but with this book, Andrew provides you with the language and tools to communicate effectively, ensuring a positive outcome for all.

Scott Burns, experienced teacher and parent

Andrew draws on his many years of experience in the education system and as a parent to provide relevant, practical information and embrace the many facets of the primary school to enable the best experience for our children and the school community.

Monique Blundell, parent

It helps to set important boundaries and provide clear direction. Trust in the school community is paramount. It is built and maintained through adherence to these boundaries and through transparent, honest collaboration.

Courtenay Smith, teacher

Refreshing emphasis on parents being the key education force in their child's life. Great tips on how parents can effectively communicate with the teachers (and vice versa) to ensure that the needs of their children are met. Strong and thought-provoking message aimed at building resilience and good character in our children.

Giovanna Sculli, parent

Contents

Foreword	ix
Acknowledgements	xi
Reflection	xiii
Introduction	1
Chapter 1: Goals of Education	5
Chapter 2: Prep Readiness	21
Chapter 3: Relationships with School Staff	31
Chapter 4: Enquiries at School	47
Chapter 5: Transitions and Milestones	65
Chapter 6: Affirmations	81
Chapter 7: Gifts for Children	91
Chapter 8: Learning at Home	103
Chapter 9: Technology	109
Chapter 10: Step Up and Be a Parent	117
Conclusion	127
Bibliography	131

Appendix 1: Parent / Volunteer Code of Conduct (extract) 135

Appendix 2: Acceptable Use of Technology and Internet Resources Consent Form 136

Appendix 3: Acceptable Use of Computer and Internet Resources 138

About the Author 141

Foreword

This book came into my possession from my priest brother in Brisbane, and I'm glad it did. The first two things to impress me were the endorsements and the fact that the author is a male principal of a Brisbane Catholic primary school. As its subtitle indicates, the book is about partnerships between parents and teachers (an approach carried out successfully in Sydney and Melbourne in recent decades by PARED—Parents in Education—schools).

The goals of the author are for children to become confident contributors to society, and for teachers and parents to engage collaboratively in their children's learning journey. The 10 chapters of this book are filled with very practical wisdom based on Andrew's 30 years of experience at the coalface dealing with children and getting parents to engage in partnerships with teachers. Long gone are the days when teachers felt that parents had done their job by bringing children into the world and delivering them to the schooling system five years later.

This book is practical and aptly illustrated to underscore its unifying theme of love, in the very everyday sense of the word. The author covers creativity, character and citizenship in some detail, touching on how parents can help prevent childhood depression and anxiety. More exercise and less screen time is the prescription, presented within the context of Maslow's well-known hierarchy of needs for a happy and healthy approach to safety and belonging. The development of a culture of trust applies not only to schools, but to any business that engages its staff in collaboration. Bottom-up suggestions in partnership with top-down inspiration are demonstrated in successful commercial organisations as well as enterprising schools.

All readers will be able to relate to the neatly explained examples, which are up-to-date in terms of what children are exposed to in the media and how adults can underestimate what children already know before their parents get around to thinking about telling them.

The author's goal in writing this book is supported by a narrative built around realistic case studies. This makes the book worthwhile reading for parents not only of primary school children, but children of any age. Even if they've left home, we all need expressions of love to be reinforced frequently and in simple ways.

Emeritus Professor Tony Shannon AM

Acknowledgements

There are numerous people who must be acknowledged for their contributions in making this book a reality. Firstly, my family: my wife Lisa, and children Zachary and Bridget. They accepted my absences when writing became a priority being juggled with work and study. Hopefully it also proved an example for teenagers who were studying at the same time.

To my friends and editors, Colleen Tracey and Allan Parker, who patiently read the original manuscripts and offered honest feedback to refine the messages—thank you.

To graphic designer Gail Semiao, whose illustrations that accompany the stories bring to life the recollections—thank you.

There are numerous other groups of people who unknowingly contributed to the message of this book. The staff at Our Lady of the Rosary School, Kenmore, where I was principal for 12 years and where a few stories were generated; my fellow principals of primary schools within the Brisbane Catholic Archdiocese; the parents at Our Lady of the Rosary School who gave feedback and provided the basis of some of my stories; and the Catholic Parents and Friends Association of Queensland.

In my career as a teacher, assistant principal and principal I have worked with thousands of families. In some small way they have each made me the educator that I am today, as our interactions have helped me upskill my working relationships with parents. While the students I first taught are now adults with their own families, some of their stories remain with me. The teachers, school officers and support staff with whom I have worked in the Catholic sector and government schools have also added to my story and this story.

Andrew Oberthur

Reflection

I dreamed I stood in a studio
And watched two sculptors there
The clay they used was a young child's mind
And they fashioned it with care.
One was a teacher; the tools being used
Were books, computers and art
One a parent with a guiding hand
And a gentle, loving heart.
Day after day the teacher toiled
With touch that was deft and sure
While the parent laboured just as hard
And polished and smoothed it o'er.
When at last their task was done
They were proud of what they'd wrought,
For the things they had moulded into the child
Could neither be sold nor bought.
And they both agreed they would have failed
If they had worked alone;
For behind the parents stood the school
And behind the teacher, the home.

'A Canopy of Stars: Some Reflections for the Journey' (Gleeson, 2018)

Introduction

I began teaching in primary schools in 1988 and became a principal in July 2001. During my 30-plus years working with children, teachers and families, I have become aware that the relationship between teachers and parents is key to achieving success for their common interest: the child.

There are lots of 'experts' giving parents advice about how to raise children. There are also just as many people giving schools and teachers advice about how they should do their job. As the father of two teenage children, I have on numerous occasions attended parenting talks to understand what the experts say about raising happy and healthy boys and girls. It was during one of these talks that I began formulating a plan to fill the gap between home and school, with adults sharing advice and working together for the benefit of children. I am indebted to my family for their encouragement and willingness to have some of their stories shared in this book.

According to researchers Henderson and Berla, 'the most accurate predictor of a student's achievement in school is not income or social status but the extent to which that student's family is able to create a home environment that encourages learning; express high (but not unrealistic) expectations for their children's achievement and future careers, and become involved in their children's education at school and in the community [sic]' (Henderson and Berla, 1994).

Teaching has changed significantly since I began in the profession many years ago. The role of parents in the education of their children continues to evolve. The demands on teachers are ever-increasing with pressure from families, government and the public. The expectations of parents have seen teachers become responsible for many things that were once family responsibilities.

Educating children needs to be a collaborative exercise between teachers and parents. In 2012, the Australian Council for Educational Research (ACER) developed a National School Improvement Tool describing nine domains towards which a school should strive in order to improve students' achievements and wellbeing. Two of the domains, Number 3 ('A Culture that Promotes Learning') and Number 9 ('School Community Partnerships'), explicitly describe the links between home and school (ACER, 2012). The ACER tool serves to reinforce the message of this book: educating children is a combined effort. Together we can make it work.

This book is based on my long experience as a teacher and principal, supported by evidence-based research where applicable, and containing references to social commentary from media, presentations and workshops by experts. It may be said that this book is a qualitative reflection on how home and school can work together for the mutual benefit of our children. It is presented in bite-sized pieces for easy reading and digestion by you: parents, carers and teachers.

In preparing the text for this book, I used the ideas garnered from the presentation I developed for parents about working with schools to strengthen the partnership. The content has had eyes cast over it by trusted friends, experienced parents, critical colleagues and a wise sage. All these people added their ideas to refine the message. The collaboration used in writing is a good example of how collective wisdom can deepen a message. The collaboration between home and school uses that collective wisdom to create environments for student success.

Each chapter will begin with the key ideas to be covered in that section. There are also personal stories gathered over my career, all based on fact. Names have been changed to keep the anonymity of all the characters. I hope you can relate to the stories. Each chapter will conclude with the key learnings identified as a summary for parents and school staff.

Recognising that there are numerous models of families in today's world, any reference to parents represents all models of parenting: Mums and Dads, single parents, same-sex couples, foster parents and any other carers who are responsible for the education and welfare of children.

As the conclusion of this book says, this isn't the final word. This means to acknowledge that the teaching profession continues to evolve, as does the role that parents play in their children's education. Some teachers say that education is cyclical, as ideas come and go. Some parents say that the engagement of parents with teachers and vice versa can only improve with time.

The message of this book is that if parents and teachers work together, the result should be children who are confident contributors to society.

I hope you enjoy this book—and feel free to give me feedback. After all, it is a key way in which we learn and improve.

1 Goals of Education

As parents, we get our children ready to start school. We pass the baton to primary school teachers, who prepare them for secondary school. Secondary school teachers in turn prepare them for tertiary studies, employment or apprenticeships. Ultimately, the goals of education should be:
- **Children who are independent, confident contributors to society**
- **Parents and teachers who trust each other and engage collaboratively in their children's learning journey**

As time flies by and our lives seemingly get busier, every moment we spend with our children is precious. 'It only seemed like yesterday that my child was still wearing nappies, and now they're at school' is something that every parent will find themselves saying. The days go fast, but we have a long journey ahead of us as we prepare our children to be well-rounded adults.

Partnership

Here's the good news: parents are not alone in this journey, and neither are teachers. If we work together, we have a better chance of moulding our children into future leaders and confident contributors to society.

Parents are our children's first educators. Whatever we do before formal schooling has a huge bearing on their preparation for primary school. I refer to the children being raised and educated as 'our' children. This acknowledges that children are the collective responsibility of their parents and their teachers. Teachers stand *in loco parentis*, in the place of a parent. Although they are part of the 'parenting' journey with the families of the children they teach, they will never replace parents.

Many researchers believe that the 'four Cs'—critical thinking, collaboration, creativity and communication—are the key to successful learning. I like the version of the 'four Cs' espoused by former Queensland Education Minister Rod Welford as the goals of education: competence, creativity, character and citizenship (Salisbury, 2011).

> **Competence:** Children should be competent in appropriate areas of learning. Australian schools are obliged to follow the Australian Curriculum to enable students to reach the achievement standards described by ACARA (the Australian Curriculum Assessment and Reporting Authority). Primary school students will have more general competencies before starting to specialise in a chosen field at secondary school.
>
> **Creativity:** Children need to engage in expressive modes of communication. Creativity can embrace many endeavours, particularly in the arts and humanities (music, dance, drama, art, media, writing, design and technology). Children should develop problem-solving and collaborative skills.
>
> **Character:** Children should learn to make wise and ethical decisions. They will try things, achieve success, make mistakes,

learn and achieve again. Through this process, we hope that they become adults of good character. My school—Our Lady of the Rosary School (OLR), Kenmore—recently redeveloped our vision statement to include this element: 'children will make wise choices, following the Gospel values'. (OLR is a Catholic school, hence the reference to the Gospel.)

Citizenship: Children should be knowledgeable of their world and be able to contribute to society. They should get involved and make a difference in their family, school and community. Programs such as the Young Rotarians provide formal opportunities in this area.

These are some of the goals of education. Now here is the challenge: guiding young people through childhood into their teenage years. Why is this so important? Here's what the experts say.

Psychologist and author Dr Judith Locke believes that children should be taught and expected to contribute to family life from as early an age as possible (Locke, 2015). Not everyone will agree with her philosophy, but children in primary school should be learning personal responsibility and how to contribute to their world and their family. Locke contends that our job as parents is to become redundant—not too soon, but soon enough. We will always love our children, but we need them to be prepared for later life.

Clinical psychologist and family therapist Andrew Fuller has discussed the role that anxiety plays in our children. His research indicates that 59 per cent of Australian children in Years 11 and 12 and 28 per cent of those in Grades 3 and 4 have clinical anxiety (Fuller, 2015).

Psychologist Dr Michael Carr-Gregg is an internationally recognised authority on teenage behaviour. He focuses on educating parents and teachers so that our young boys of today won't turn into the lazy lads he suspects they are becoming (Carr-Gregg & Robinson, 2017). I will dare to make the generalisation that our young women may also be heading in a questionable direction. Steve Biddulph, psychologist and author of *Raising Boys* and *Raising Girls,* emphasises that we need to break this cycle to produce young people who will contribute to society (Biddulph, 2019).

There is a trend appearing here. Parents and schools need to work together to ensure a safe future in the hands of our young people. We are responsible for giving children the skills to thrive.

Slow Parenting

I have watched families grow up, and the beginning of my teaching career in 1988 seems like only yesterday. I am now working with parents who were once my students!

London-based slow-movement ambassador Carl Honoré specialises in a niche area of 'slow-change' parenting (Honoré, 2009 and 2010). Slow parenting is about quality time with our children. Slowing down is difficult for parents who are driven to provide their children with many opportunities for success at school and beyond. Parents who have timetabled their children's lives by providing numerous extra activities may find additional time unoccupied by organised events quite challenging. Some may argue that keeping children occupied means less opportunity for mischief. There is some merit to that notion. However, children who haven't learnt to occupy themselves from a young age may get into serious mischief when they do have free time as teens and young adults!

Some families engage tutors for their primary school children. Then there are sport and musical commitments, along with other creative pursuits. Parents want the best for their children and believe they can help them by scheduling extracurricular activities. No argument there, but let's allow children to relax. It is about having balance in our lives. We need time to connect with our children, and they need time to connect with us. One-on-one time is important for the parent and the child. It is often a rare and valuable treat to share such time, which can re-establish the bonds shared during the child's early formative years.

Let Them Be Kids

Schools are increasingly collecting and using data on things like academic performance and attendance records. Parents want to know a school's academic results, which are becoming more publicly available. But schools are about more than just academic outputs. As goes the saying often misattributed to Einstein: 'Not everything that can be counted counts, and not everything that counts can be counted' (Cameron, 1963). Schools are responsible for many pursuits beyond academic excellence, including the development of qualities such as self-regulation and resilience. We want all children to learn and improve. We want to educate them socially, physically, emotionally, creatively and— in the case of faith-based schools—spiritually.

It is important for children to have the free play time that will allow them to be creative, solve problems and manage their social interactions. Children need to learn to take risks and explore the world on their own terms. They should learn to be self-sufficient and occupy their time without adults having to manage and plan every minute of the day.

It is also important for parents to slow down and make time for ourselves. This gives us breathing space away from the timetabled life of running after children. We can demonstrate to them the necessity of downtime for recharging our batteries.

Switching Off

In 2014, Carl Honoré was invited to do a social experiment with four Australian families who led busy timetabled lives. The outcomes of this experiment were broadcast in the 2015 television show *Frantic Family Rescue*. One simple idea that Honoré promoted was the reduction of screen time for all family members. This meant less television-watching and less use of mobile devices. The idea proved a challenge (no one said it would be easy) but there were some excellent social and physical reasons behind the practice. Screen time means less social engagement and face-to-face communication, less outdoor play and recreation, less exercise. Screen time late at night stimulates the brain and makes going to sleep more difficult. When there is less screen time, children engage in conversation and learn social skills through playing family games.

When time usually spent on screens is used for exercise, we have fitter and healthier children. This time can also be used for sleepovers, family games and other activities for which we are often too busy. Teenagers require approximately 8–10 hours of sleep, while young children require 10–12 hours. They need to let their minds and bodies rest, and so do their parents.

Removing or minimising the use of a mobile phone for a teenager, or even a younger child, may feel like you are cutting off their main form of engagement with their peers and the world. I am reasonably confident that they may rebel and object at the thought of such a practice, as their phone is often seen as their lifeline. (How did we ever survive without our mobile phones?) But it will bring long-term benefits such as improved engagement with family and better face-to-face communication skills. I am not saying stop all screen time. Watching television and engaging with peers through mobile phones and social networking is completely fine—in moderation and under supervision.

> *The successful warrior is the average man with laser-like focus.*
>
> *Bruce Lee*

Children's Needs

Abraham Maslow introduced his concept of a hierarchy of needs in his 1943 paper 'A Theory of Human Motivation' (Maslow, 1943). This hierarchy suggests that we are motivated to fulfil basic needs before moving to more advanced needs. To grow into a happy and healthy person, a child needs to be safe and to belong. Children also need food, shelter and clothing. Once they have the basics, they can learn. These essentials should ideally be provided by parents and carers, although schools may be called upon to contribute under some circumstances.

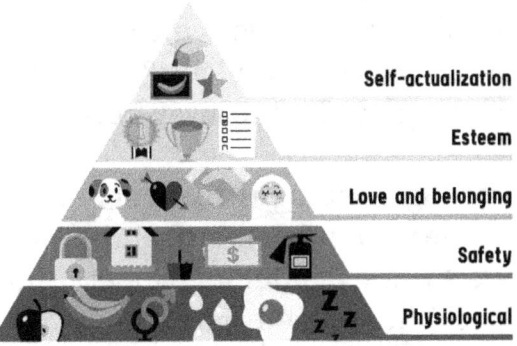

Independence

Now let's start on the things we can do together to build children's independence. Some are parental responsibilities and some are the duties of the school. Before children come to school, they should be able to do the following.

> **Dress themselves:** Children should be able to do their own buttons, tie their shoelaces, put on their jumpers and recognise their name on their uniform. Parents should engage with fun activities and games that encourage fine motor skills.
>
> **Eat independently:** Children should be able to open their lunch boxes, containers, packets, straws and anything else they use for lunch. Nude food (food without wrappers, often fruit and vegetables) makes life much easier and is healthier. Although schools may have policies on healthy food, these are often very difficult to police. Remember, schools can't always regulate parents' choices and decisions.

Toilet themselves: Children should be independent before they get to school. At enrolment interviews, I ask parents if their child is toilet trained. Does the child have or need spare underpants, just in case of accidents? Having to assist with the toileting of children takes time away from the core business of school staff.

Manage personal hygiene: Children should be able to use tissues and wash their hands. Older boys and girls will need to start using deodorant. Upper primary girls need to have a 'girl pack' (feminine hygiene pack), possibly disguised in a pencil case or similar bag. It is not uncommon for girls in primary school to get their periods, so they must be able to manage when they do.

To complement these life skills, I recommend that children be familiar with the following.

Money: Awareness of currency. Even though many adults live in their own cashless world of credit cards and electronic transfers, children still need to understand and use cash.

Time: Awareness of analogue and digital clocks and watches. Schools will teach children how to read clocks, but their initial engagement should be at home.

Shapes and colours: Observation and memorisation of common shapes and colours that we see in everyday life. Children learn through engagement and there are so many life lessons in the world.

Communication: Speaking confidently, using good manners (greeting people, saying please and thank you) and showing courtesy to those they meet. The ability to talk and engage with people starts in infancy and is enhanced with every opportunity for social interaction.

Managing their own belongings: Allow your child to carry their own school bag. They should be expected to pack and unpack their bag. Make sure to label everything with your child's name. If they lose something, they should try to find it. If the possession cannot be found, your child should pay for its replacement by doing additional chores. If we replace items without a consequence, we develop a culture of disposable commodities. Supervise your children while they pack their bags for camps and sleepovers. They will work out what to wear and how much they can carry.

When your child leaves something behind at home or at school, how do you respond? If it is an important item such as an assignment, then support your child by getting it for them if possible. Add a polite, calm reminder that this was their responsibility. If it is a less important item, leave it. Missing out or experiencing a consequence won't hurt a child and they may learn from it.

First Impressions

Both parents and teachers may have terms of endearment (nicknames) for children. Such terms often reflect a physical or emotional characteristic of the child. Nicknames build rapport between children and adults. A word of caution: please make children's nicknames positive, especially if they are used in public. The potential negative impact of nicknames is not something we want to promote.

> *" Our self-image is formed from our family and school ties. "*
>
> *Michael Grinder*

In my first year of teaching, I was introduced to a child whose mother had given her the nickname 'Mad Jan'. Straight away that gave me an impression of the girl's potentially negative behaviour. Thirty years later I came across a mother who nicknamed her son 'Devil'. These nicknames can become self-fulfilling prophecies. Mums and Dads, any nicknames you choose for your children need to be positive or at least neutral. Do not give them nicknames with negative connotations!

Trust Between Parents and Teachers

Throughout their primary schooling, your children will experience some brilliant teachers and some average teachers. How they cope and adapt is critical. There are various things that will challenge parents' trust of their child's school. A keen topic of discussion is the optimal number of children in a class. Class size in fact has limited impact on student achievement, as identified by educational researcher John Hattie (Hattie, 2009). The impact on student achievement when classes vary from 25–28 and 27–30 students is negligible. Classes of approximately 17 would be ideal but are financially unsustainable in most schools. The quality of the teacher and their pedagogy (how they teach) are more important. Schools are full of social interactions and not everything will work in every school—context is relevant. Teachers need to 'know thy impact' on student work and achievement (Hattie, 2009). Principals need to give teachers permission to stop doing things that are discretionary and have no impact on learning (what I call 'froth and bubble'). The shared priority of parents and principals should be to get the best teachers in front of children. Those teachers who need upskilling should be supported to improve their work.

While I have emphasised the importance of teacher–parent relationships, other generations also have important roles to play in children's educational journeys. It is not uncommon for grandparents to attend enrolment interviews, orientation sessions and Grandparents' Days, as well as dropping off and picking up grandchildren.

I have met some real characters of grandparents: their own children went to their grandchildren's school, so they remember the 'good old days'; some have fascinating pasts including living through eras of political corruption. Some live overseas and are just visiting; some care for their grandchildren when their children are incapable of doing so. Regardless of their stories, grandparents have an important place in the lives of grandchildren and school staff need to embrace the relationship.

Honesty Is the Best Policy

Parents and caring adults should encourage young people to have a go at anything that stimulates their interests. All too quickly, children will grow into teenagers and then adults. Exposure to a variety of opportunities may help them uncover their passions and talents.

Not everything a child explores will go according to plan. There will be breakages, both literal and figurative. Children should be encouraged to explore within reasonable bounds of safety. Parents should consider personal safety but keep breakages in perspective. As the saying goes, there's no use in crying over spilt milk.

Children need to know the truth about their abilities. They should be supported but grounded with honesty. As parents and teachers, we face a balancing act in encouraging our children while being realistic in our appraisal. We can certainly give children aspirations to achieve greatness and don't need to put limits on their potential. However, we need to be realistic. Very few children will make it to the Olympics; very few will make a living out of playing sport or music. From what I hear at enrolment interviews, it appears that most children are gifted— yet research says that only 10 per cent of the student population may have some gifts (Carmody, 2018). Very few children are naturally gifted or will make a living out of their gifts. Many children will continue to enjoy sport and music long into adult life. Many will be highly successful in their chosen field. But most children between the ages of 4 and 12 have no idea how their lives will evolve. They deserve our honest guidance.

What does honesty look like? It means praising children's efforts when warranted. It means encouraging them to try hard in all they do. It means telling them that they can be what they want to be if their talents and effort lead them down the right path. It means giving feedback on their behaviour and skills, rather than who they are as people.

What does it not look like? It means not telling children that they will be world-beaters. It means not telling all who will listen how fabulous your children are. Be proud, not boastful. Nobody wants to hear how everyone else's children are more brilliant than their own.

Teaching Resilience

I have worked with children in upper primary school who have rarely, if ever, made a mistake or been in trouble. The first time is shocking for them. I have seen children 'fail' on the sporting arena and dissolve into a tearful mess. While we don't want children to fall down, it is better that they do so in a safe and supportive environment rather than as teenagers or university students facing more significant consequences.

Those lessons in life may be scary, but they are necessary. Children need to learn from their failings, get back up and start again. Children who do not overcome perfectionist tendencies may find life hard. Life is not black and white—it is sometimes very grey.

A Grade Five girl was in my office. Her parents were concerned that their daughter was stressed about 'getting in trouble' with her class teacher, as it was the first time that she had made a big enough mistake to warrant it. After I invited the girl and her mother to discuss this with the class teacher, they realised an important lesson in life: it's OK to make mistakes and learn from them. Bouncing back from such lessons is an indicator of a child's resilience.

All children will experience a variety of friendship groups and social dynamics. These will hopefully be with peers whose families value education and believe in their children's potential. When friendships change, our children may be hurt but they need to get up again. At these times they may feel lost and vulnerable, unable to navigate the social maze of peer interactions. They will need their parents and teachers to listen and provide reassurance.

Learn from Every Experience

It is important that parents and teachers embrace the philosophy that each day is a new day. Mistakes will be dealt with on the day they occur, and children can arrive at school the next day starting afresh. The consequence for the misdemeanour may have to be carried over into the second day, but children should come to school knowing that they are in a safe environment. Teachers who have this philosophy should be applauded, and I encourage all parents and teachers to know that children will make mistakes. They are imperfect human beings, as are we.

Children should be able to name caring adults who believe in them and give them confidence that they will be successful. They must be able to trust their teachers and see that they highly value learning, progress and excellence. Teachers should model these qualities. They can do this by talking about their progress in continuing to learn about how and what to teach, or by sharing knowledge and techniques gained in professional development courses. This indicates to their students that learning is an ongoing, lifelong experience.

During their formative years, children are most influenced by parents and teachers. Together we can make a difference. These pages should provide you with new ideas and give you the courage to experiment. There is no one manual for parenting—it is a tough gig.

LESSONS LEARNED

Parents Please:

Trust your children's teachers

Engage your children with life skills

Provide the essentials for your children

Have confidence in your children, allowing them to experiment and learn

Teachers Please:

Be empathetic

Be courageous and determined

Model lifelong learning

2 Prep Readiness

When preparing for the start of school, we must ensure that:
- Children are equipped with the life skills that will allow them to learn
- Teachers can concentrate on their core business of teaching the Australian Curriculum

The education of children, especially young children, is the collaborative responsibility of parents and teachers. Both groups want children to have the best start to school. The foundational years in early childhood education set children up for success.

There are four areas that parents should address in the weeks leading up to their children starting school for the very first time:

- Independence
- Communication
- Social skills
- Motor skills

Let me stress that the acquisition of the skills and experiences under each of these categories is not equivalent to an entrance exam. Teachers will teach all children at whichever skill level they have.

Independence

It is important that children have a degree of independence when they arrive at school. Certain life skills will allow them to feel comfortable and confident in themselves as they navigate the demands of school. I encourage you to do a mental audit to ascertain if your child has the following skills:

Can they toilet themselves independently? Can they dress themselves independently, managing zips and buttons and shoelaces? If they can't manage shoelaces, I would advise that they wear Velcro shoes initially. Can they recognise their own printed name, and hence identify their belongings that will have been labelled by their parents? Can they carry their own bag in and out of school?

Can your child pack and unpack their own bag? Can they use tissues independently? There is nothing more frustrating for a teacher particularly during the cold and flu season, than to have to assist children to blow their noses hygienically!

Can your child manage eating and drinking independently? This includes opening and closing their lunchboxes and drink bottles, as well as opening poppers (drink cartons). If you are going to buy your child a new lunchbox, take them to the shops with you and have them test out the lunchboxes. Although it may be tempting to surprise them with a new lunchbox, it will become a task beyond their means if they can't use it independently.

Communication

Let's now explore some of the basic communication skills that are necessary to give children a degree of confidence and competence when they start school. Can your child make their needs known by asking simple questions such as 'May I go to the bathroom please' and 'May I have a drink of water please'? Can they use appropriate greetings such as 'Good morning', 'Good afternoon' and 'Hello, my name is...'? Can they speak in sentences that are more than two or three words long? Do they maintain eye contact when having a conversation with their peers and with the staff around them? Can your child take their turn in a conversation? Do they wait for the other person to respond and can they engage in a two-person or even three-person conversation? Can your child talk about a subject of interest? Is their articulation clear and can they be understood? Do they pronounce words at an age-appropriate level?

According to research, children don't have to know all their sounds until approximately seven years of age (Kid Sense, 2021). Only seven per cent of our communication comes through the words we say, while the remaining 93 per cent comes from vocal variation and non-verbal cues (Advaney, 2017). However, children's communication relies heavily on the spoken word until they develop the ability to read and interpret non-verbal cues.

Equally important are the child's diction and ability to pronounce words correctly. Starting school at approximately the age of five, children are not expected to have perfect articulation and pronunciation. For example, it is common for them to pronounce 'th' as 'f', saying 'Fursday' instead of 'Thursday'. Another common mispronunciation is replacing the 'y' in yellow with an 'l'. Children often have a rolling 'r', saying 'wed' instead of 'red'. These examples of a child's language development can be monitored and corrected by parents very early on without any significant speech intervention. You can help your child develop language skills by correcting their speech in a fun way and affirming the right pronunciation. Break up words into smaller patterns: yes > yet > yep > yell > and then 'yellow'. (Please note that I am not a speech therapist, just a principal who has listened to many children over the years.) Don't neglect to correct poor articulation or pronunciation that you find endearing. What appears cute now will no longer be desirable by the time speech patterns are highly developed at the age of 15 or 16. Language development is easier to change the earlier it is worked on.

Social Skills

Can your child share? Can they take turns? Can they listen? Do they know how to enter social networks with children and adults? Can they play games and accept losing? Are they given boundaries around their amount of screen time at home? At school they certainly will be. Do they comply with the behavioural expectations of their parents and preschool teachers? These skills indicate children's ability to attend to learning at school.

Motor Skills

Let's first explore the big body movements known as gross motor skills. Mastery of these larger movements allows children to address their fine motor skills, the smaller movements of manipulating things with the hands and fingers. Can your child run, jump, hop, skip, climb? Do they have the core strength to sit for a few minutes on the floor or a chair without slouching or lying down? Can they throw and catch? Can they use monkey bars? Although the ability to use monkey bars is not a necessity, it demonstrates the child's core strength. It's also an indication of their ability to cross the midline, the imaginary line down the centre of our body. When walking up and down stairs, do they put one foot after the other instead of placing each foot on the same step? Children can build gross motor skills by playing outdoors, exploring parks and using playgrounds. These activities give them a natural strength that will hold them in good stead as they enter school.

Fine motor skills allow children to use their hands in specific ways. Can your child hold their pencil correctly? Can they open the lids of glue sticks? Can they manipulate blocks and Lego? Can they use scissors? Can they thread beads? Are they happy to colour inside the lines of a drawing? When they use a keyboard and other technologies, are they competent?

By working on these four sets of skills with your children, you will help them to feel confident and competent when they start school. Your child's mastery of these skills will also assure teachers that they don't have to worry about doing up shoelaces, opening lunchboxes, toileting them or helping them blow their nose.

There are other skills that will be an advantage in your child's learning of the curriculum: counting; knowing the alphabet, colours and shapes; and writing their name.

Some other tips to prepare a child for the transition to school include:
- Trying on their uniform—especially shoes—a week or two before school starts
- Visiting school (most schools will have an orientation program)
- Meeting with classmates if possible.

Age, Sex and School Readiness

'My son's birthday falls a couple of months prior to the cut-off date for him to start school. I think I will give him a second year at kindy.' I have heard these comments many times as a primary school principal. They have prompted me to analyse the factors that contribute to parents' and educators' determination of a child's readiness to start school. Is this readiness determined by the child's age and sex? I think not! There is a general belief that boys should have a second year of kindergarten to assist them. This decision should be made by looking at the individual child's competencies. There is no perfect process to determine a child's readiness to start school.

At the outset, let me live on the edge by making some assumptions:
- Parents and educators want what is best for children
- Parents know their children in the home and social setting
- Parents are the first educators of their children
- Educators have the training and knowledge to formally teach children
- Early childhood educators prepare children to start school.

For a child to be successful in their first year at school, they will ideally have age-appropriate communication, socialisation and independence skills. I have met mature four-year-old boys who were ready for school. I have also met immature five-year-old girls who struggled when they started school. Age and sex are only a couple of factors that parents and educators must consider when determining if a child is ready.

If determining the best age for a child to start school was easy, then there would be a consistent age and criteria set for parents and educators to follow. In Australia, each state determines how old a child must be to start school. The states also determine if a child can start school early. These recommendations differ not just from state to state, but also from country to country. With our world being increasingly accessible (pre- and hopefully post-pandemic), a percentage of families have their children educated in more than one state and occasionally more than one country.

A child's communication, socialisation and independence will be influenced by the experiences provided by parents, carers and early childhood educators.

Communication for a four- or five-year-old child includes expressive language (the ability to express themselves and make their needs known through speech). It also includes receptive language (the ability to follow instructions and comprehend). Speech and language skills are important communication skills. You can build a key aspect of your child's development by exposing them to letters, words, stories and literature.

Socialisation for a four- or five-year-old child is the ability to mix with their peers and practise behaviours that promote social engagement in an age-appropriate way. Practices include sharing, waiting, taking turns, joining groups and making friends; all important skills for engaging at school and successfully learning.

Independence skills for a four- or five-year-old child include the ability to manage themselves with life skills at an age-appropriate level. These skills may include dressing and feeding themselves, looking after their belongings, recognising their name and carrying their school bag.

Other Conditions and Considerations

There are many conditions that provide children with the experiences to prepare them for school. These must be considered when determining if a child is ready to start school.

Children who have been in an early childhood setting since they were a few months old will have had experiences that other children may not have. They may have gained important communication, socialisation and independence skills, along with exposure to literacy and numeracy foundations. Social settings such daycare and kindergarten offer the opportunity to share, wait, take turns, make friends and join groups. Parents who don't send their children to daycare or kindergarten should provide social experiences in other settings: it's important that children have opportunities to meet, play and engage with others their own age.

Children who have siblings may have experiences at home that an only child does not. Eldest, youngest and middle children are all exposed to unique experiences. The eldest child may be more independent if their parents are busy with younger siblings. Conversely, they may receive less parental bonding time and exposure to literacy-building materials if their parents are too busy.

Only children may have parents who spend more time with them, giving them the foundational skills necessary for school. Living in an adult world may mean greater exposure to language and communication. It may mean less exposure to social environments with peers.

Children with parents who both work may have different experiences to children who have one or both parents at home for most of the week.

Children whose parents believe in negotiating with them and giving them autonomy for their decisions may have difficulties coping with structure. School is a setting where rules are designed to keep all students safe and must be followed with minimal debate and negotiation.

Children whose parents value literacy, numeracy, language and communication development will have stronger foundations for learning.

The **genetic make-up of a child** will also have an influence on their readiness. The debate about nature (genetics) versus nurture (upbringing) is relevant when determining a child's readiness for school.

The **cultural background of a child** may also influence their foundational skills and experiences relevant to school. Some cultures have different beliefs about early childhood education, or how parents should 'raise' their children. This may influence the child's exposure to their native tongue or to the language in which they will be taught.

Transition and orientation programs also influence a child's readiness for school. Some schools are introducing School Readiness programs to ensure that children and parents are as ready as possible to start school. Such programs are designed to give children a brief experience of Prep and to allow school staff to observe them.

Kindergarten educators provide transition statements that give parents and primary school staff an indication of the child's readiness for school. Primary school staff are encouraged to discuss each child with the feeder kindergarten staff.

What this indicates is that numerous factors influence a child's grounding in communication, socialisation and independence, all necessary to support success in school. Parents and educators need to make informed decisions.

LESSONS LEARNED

Parents Please:

Give your children opportunities to practise skills for success

Talk with your child's preschool or kindergarten teacher

Try not to compare children's development

Teachers Please:

Avoid making generalisations about student readiness

Be transparent in processes

Listen to parents, and especially to the concerns of first-time parents

3 Relationships with School Staff

For many parents, the primary school journey will be new and their first return since they left their own school several decades ago.

This chapter will explore how school personnel and parents can build relationships and then work together for the benefit of their children. (Remember, they are 'our' children, cared for by a community!)

I will discuss how and why parents communicate with various members of the school staff. We will see examples of effective and respectful communication that builds a culture of trust and collaboration.

School Secretaries

The first people you will meet are the secretaries, who are perceived to 'run the school'. Often the secretaries are the voice and face of the school, the people who make initial contact with parents. This is where a culture of trust can begin. As a parent, you should feel that you can trust the school after initial contact.

Secretaries should be responsive to your enrolment enquiries. The tone of their response will give an initial impression of the school and its culture. As a principal I hope (and often pray) that my secretaries 'sell' the school with their friendly demeanour. The secretaries will pride themselves on being responsive and will promote the school as an environment that can meet the needs of your children. Should you have a query that can't be addressed by the secretaries, it is their responsibility to pass it on to a staff member who can provide the answers. Once your family is part of the school community, there will be numerous times that the school may need to contact you.

Secretaries may have to call you for a variety of reasons. The best will begin the call by saying something along the lines of 'Hi Mr or Mrs Smith, it is Jill here from your child's school. Everything is OK with your child. I just need to talk to you about...' You are immediately reassured that everything is fine and that the school is being communicative about something necessary.

When you get such a phone call from a school secretary, please understand that they are calling you in the best interests of your child. There are occasions when parents aren't always gracious in their response to the secretary's call. They are not calling to interrupt your meeting, tennis game or shopping trip; they are calling because they care. Reasons for secretaries to call include your child being sick, a form needing to be returned promptly or a change in school plans to which you need to be alerted.

There may also be occasions when you call the school and seek assistance, guidance or counsel. A secretary is likely to be your first respondent. How you communicate may affect the quality of the response you receive. A highly professional staff member will be pleasant and efficient. Ideally the response will be articulate and helpful. Let's run through some probable scenarios of communication from home to school.

Scenario 1: Parent calls up to explain that their child is sick and asks if work could be emailed home by the teacher.

The secretary thanks the parent for the information, tells them that the message will be passed on, asks them to email the teacher directly, and reassures them that they will hear from the teacher within the length of time specified by school protocols. They finally wish the child a speedy recovery. This exchange has built a culture of trust in a few brief moments.

Scenario 2: Parent seeks advice about repeating their child.

The secretary thanks the parent for trusting the school with their child's continuing education. They reassure them that the school will walk the educational journey with the family. They then make an appointment for the parents to meet with the relevant staff to guide them in their decision.

Scenario 3: Parent seeks advice about good future schools for either secondary education or even a move elsewhere in primary school (for example, if the family is relocating).

The response from the secretary may vary depending on their personal experience and current knowledge. Do they know high schools in the local area? Did their own children go to school locally? Do they have knowledge of schools in other areas? The message should be the same: we will assist you to find the best school for your child beyond our own school.

You may be asking why we would bother assisting families who are leaving! There is one key reason: parents are often the best advocates for a school. I have enrolled families from the other side of the world on the recommendation of current or past school families. Expats working overseas and parents whose jobs require frequent relocations have networks of family and friends. Social media allows complete strangers to seek opinions from likeminded parents. Parents are some of our greatest advocates and we are well-served in assisting them to move happily from our environment to the next. Let's be honest: when parents get together, they discuss school life and staff. How about we work together on this!

Scenario 4: A parent complains about the school's poor communication or about the poor results of their child.

This is often the most challenging time for the secretary. Parents may be uncomfortable receiving negative feedback, even though it may not be directed at them. So, what can the secretary do? This may sound silly, but it is important: they can thank the parent for bringing their concern to the attention of the school, as it is through their feedback that the school can improve (even if the complaint is unwarranted or unreasonable). I am not saying that the customer is always right. The secretary might direct the parent to the staff member best placed to respond to their concerns. They will then reassure the parent that they will have heard from the relevant staff member within a given timeframe. If the parent remains agitated or expects answers immediately, then hopefully the principal will have counselled the secretary on how to handle the situation.

The secretary should write down the feedback and summarise it back to the parent so that they feel heard. If staff respond in a positive and helpful manner, the frustrated parent may begin to mirror this energy. If communication is not as positive as it could be, then either parent or secretary needs the skills to keep the conversation neutral or, better still, turn it into a positive. Both parents and secretaries should remember that you catch more flies with honey than vinegar!

A culture of trust should be established by school secretary and parents at initial contact. Both parties should strive to be open, honest and positive in their communication styles.

Leadership Team

You will probably meet the principal or another member of the leadership team at your child's enrolment interview. Meeting the principal or deputy principal is an opportunity to build rapport, ask questions and establish protocols and expectations. Here's where the trust is strengthened, assuming that the school secretary has done a good job in welcoming the family to the school community.

A principal is likely to greet a family by name, with a warm smile and a matching handshake. Ideally, they will greet the child at eye height. The child can also be greeted with a friendly gesture such as a high-five. Parents can prepare their child by practising the principal's name so that the child can appropriately respond to their welcome.

During the enrolment interview, it is likely that the principal will ask parents questions about their child. Some schools prefer the child to be present to do simple screening tests with another member of staff. The principal may also engage with the child, asking them questions about kindergarten or their current school. Other questions about the child's interests should engage the child and provide the principal with more pieces of the puzzle.

A tour of the school is another opportunity to build rapport. Whichever staff member leads the tours can enhance the culture of trust and build rapport between home and school. An exploration of common interests and a welcoming, friendly smile will help the family relax and embrace the opportunities that the school can provide.

Parents need to feel comfortable and confident that the school can meet the needs of their child. To this end, the principal should be prepared to respond to parents' questions about the school and the educational journey of their child. These questions may cover a broad range of topics, including:
- What are the strengths of the school?
- What are the plans for the school?
- How do teachers cope with the variety of demands placed on them, including the need to differentiate the curriculum for the variety of learners in the class?

- What learning support is available for children verified with a disability?
- How is the school performing academically?
- Which extracurricular opportunities are available to children?
- What is the school's philosophy on bullying?
- How can parents be involved in the school?
- What are the school's expectations of parents?
- What are the school's guidelines on homework?
- How does the school teach reading, phonics, literacy etc.?

At religious schools (with examples especially pertaining to Catholic schools), questions may include:
- Our family is not Catholic. Will that affect our enrolment in a Catholic school?
- What is the school's relationship with the parish?
- How are sacraments celebrated in the community?

Confident and honest responses will build rapport and trust between the parents and the school leadership. Honesty can be offered from two contexts: an explanation of the governing authority's official position on a topic (homework, standardised testing results), and a personal opinion giving families reassurance that the principal understands their view of the world. If a principal doesn't have an answer for a parent's question, they should feel confident enough to say so and commit to getting back to the parent within a given timeframe.

The principal should also invite further questions from parents after the enrolment interview. It is common for parents to remember questions once they walk out the school gate. Parents may email or call with questions to which the school will respond.

It is also important that parents give honest answers when responding to a principal's questions. Whether the principal is asking the parent to describe their child (not every child is a genius) or enquiring about a family's capacity to meet financial obligations, an honest response is necessary. Although these may initially be uncomfortable conversations, they are easier than the alternative of having a discussion after problems have arisen.

Working Together as One

One of the greatest lessons for parents and principals is that they are on an educational journey together and have the best interests of the child at heart. Education relies on parents and school staff working together! Both parties need to accept that the journey may not be perfect. Education revolves around human beings with flaws and imperfections. There will be teachers whose teaching style matches a student's learning style almost perfectly. There will be perfect parents for some teachers. There will be perfect years. However, we rarely live in an ideal world. Cooperation is the key to success.

Teachers

Once your child has been assigned to a class, their teacher will become the most important person in their life and yours at school. Parents and teachers should work together to develop protocols and expectations. This is where and how trust deepens. Early in the school year, teachers will establish their communication protocols with parents. This will usually involve an exchange of email addresses so that teachers can keep parents informed of what's happening around the school, particularly in the child's class. It also allows parents to inform the teachers of anything happening in their child's life that may affect their ability to learn and function as effectively as possible. Teachers will also have access to parents' telephone numbers. If a teacher calls you, please be open to their communication. The teacher, if they are diplomatic and sensitive, may begin the conversation by saying something along the lines of 'Everything is OK at school. I just need to talk to you about...' This usually means that you can relax and engage in conversation about the issue. Hopefully the teacher will occasionally ring with some good news as well, or with some information that will help your child on their learning journey.

Communication Considerations

Communication from teachers to parents will continue on a semi-regular basis as needed to support the child's education. Formal parent-teacher interviews focusing on the child's academic progress take place once or twice a year. In some schools, students may lead these conversations. These may need to happen more frequently depending upon the child's learning needs and the goals collaboratively set by parents and teachers.

Teachers may email parents an invitation to discuss their child's behaviour. Sometimes these conversations may address challenging behaviours that need support from home and school. This collaboration is critical to keep the child on track to maximise their learning opportunities. There may be occasions where a teacher invites a parent to talk about the social dynamics related to their child's behaviour. Parents may ask to see teachers for similar matters, especially if a child is concerned about friendship groups. It may be necessary for a parent to ask a teacher for insight into how their child is socially progressing.

I believe that it is good to avoid surprises here. Parents should inform teachers if something is going to affect their child's ability to attend to learning. Conversely, if parents are not fully aware of what is happening to their child at school, it is the responsibility of the teachers to inform them. If something is distressing a child at school, the teacher could send an email or make a quick phone call to inform the parents and advise them that they will monitor and support the child as best they can.

There will be situations that distract a child from learning. Examples include relocation, parental separation and the death of a pet. I would encourage parents to inform the teacher so that they can monitor the child and be conscious of changes in the child's demeanour. This reinforces Hattie's assertion that the two most important people in a child's primary school education are the child themselves and their teacher (Hattie, 2009). The relationship between teachers and parents is therefore critical to building a culture of trust, collaboration and enquiry.

Relationships with School Staff

> *" Surprise is the enemy of confidence. "*
>
> Michael Grinder

How to Build or Not Build Rapport

The rapport that teachers develop with students and parents is critical in building a culture of trust. How teachers go about building that rapport will depend on their personality and experiences. Teachers need to know their impact on a child's learning (Hattie, 2009). Acknowledging that every child is different allows teachers to build rapport differently from child to child. Some children will be very emotionally intelligent and appreciate a teacher's humour. Others may lack such a level of emotional intelligence and hence may not understand the humour. Teachers should be very cautious about how they build rapport with students and should especially avoid sarcasm.

> *I once saw a teacher use sarcastic humour in front of a student and their parents. The parents and the student laughed it off and enjoyed the friendly banter because they obviously had a rapport with that teacher. Within a matter of days, I saw the same teacher use very similar sarcasm in an attempt to build rapport with a different student in front of one of their parents. This parent didn't understand the attempt at humour, took great offence and proceeded to make an appointment to see the principal—me—for an explanation and to request that the teacher be reminded of their professional boundaries. This attempt to build rapport through humour worked for one family, but was misdirected for another family. I advise*

teachers to avoid using sarcasm as it may be misinterpreted. Using it as a rapport technique is high-risk and will likely only succeed with those who use sarcasm themselves.

Specialist Teacher Relationships

Your child will encounter teachers who specialise in areas such as music, languages and physical education. You can build a relationship with each of these teachers as the need arises. A specialist teacher may contact you about a sports carnival or a creative event. They may wish to discuss your child's outstanding skillset, their behaviour, or additional work necessary to get them up to speed. They may have identified an exceptional talent that needs fostering, or they may need to discuss your child's reluctance to participate. If this is the case, please be open to the feedback.

You may be invited to get involved in activities such as sports carnivals or excursions. Again, the more involved you are in your child's education, the better their achievements will be.

As you can see, the relationship between teachers and parents is critical and will hopefully be very positive from the outset. If the relationship declines or communication fails, schools have support mechanisms by which rapport may be repaired. Children attend primary school for 10 months out of every year. This is a significant length of time through which they need to be supported, and thus the relationship between home and school must be enhanced for success.

Building Relationships with Non-Teaching Staff, or Not

School officers (teachers' aides) may be working in your child's classroom. It is unusual and not recommended that parents develop a professional relationship with the school officers, who work under the guidance of the teaching staff. If your child's class has the support of a school officer or other caring adult, your child will possibly develop a relationship with that person.

If this is the case, it is still recommended that all communication go via the teacher. The school officer works under instruction. They are not responsible for teaching, planning, assessing or reporting on progress. School officers nonetheless play important roles in the lives of children. They also play an important role by supporting the teachers to ensure that all children can access the curriculum. The rapport that school officers have with students and teachers can be very important in building trust and collaboration.

Learning Support Teachers

Working alongside classroom teachers and school officers are the learning support teachers, sometimes called support teachers for inclusive education and historically called remedial teachers. These teachers play a key role in ensuring that all children can access the curriculum through differentiation, individualised programs, goal-setting and resourcing. They also case-manage children with significant needs.

Parents should be informed when support teachers are engaged with their child. Support teachers frequently work inside the classroom, often with small groups. They may also model lessons for class teachers or co-teach after co-planning. The class teacher is thus supported to meet the needs of learners at both ends of the academic spectrum.

Historically, learning support teachers worked with children who struggled with their academic progress. There is now also a focus on meeting the needs of high achievers. Some schools employ teachers for gifted-and-talented programs. If this is not possible, then the learning support teacher is the ideal person to help the class teacher differentiate the curriculum.

If your child is being helped by a learning support teacher, this does not mean they have a significant learning deficit. It means that their class teacher has the expert advice and support of a colleague to advance the learning of all students independent of their starting point. Support teachers also work very closely with school officers. They often guide the school officer's work, planning the intervention necessary to support children. A culture of collaboration is reinforced among teaching staff and support staff, as well as with parents.

Specialists in Emotional Support

Working alongside teachers are guidance counsellors. If your child's teacher recommends the guidance counsellor's involvement, then please appreciate that their rationale for doing so is the welfare and wellbeing of your child. Guidance counsellors are playing a growing role in the lives of children in schools. Children frequently need more emotional support than they did in previous years. Please embrace the support that a guidance counsellor may be providing for your child.

A recommendation to a guidance counsellor is not a crisis point, but an indicator that your child may benefit from additional emotional support and guidance. Having said that, they may have significant needs that require support from a guidance counsellor. A counsellor planning to engage with your child will contact you to get some background on the needs that have been identified. They will explain their role, develop a rapport with you and then develop a rapport with your child. If they give a referral, they will recommend mechanisms and specialists by which your child will get the necessary further support. We are working in support of your child's learning journey, which may be affected by their emotional welfare. We thus draw on the expertise of a guidance counsellor to enhance your child's ability to learn and perform to their potential and beyond.

Medical and Allied Health Specialists

Teachers may also recommend medical investigation that can lead to intervention. This process may involve occupational therapists (OTs), physiotherapists, paediatric assessments or tests for speech, hearing or vision. As always, the motivator is the welfare and wellbeing of your child. Experience tells me that children are often coming to school with fewer abilities than those demonstrated by their counterparts of many years ago. As such, many schools now invest in screening tests (screeners). These are minor tests that are conducted by the school or by occupational therapists, through which a holistic view of a child may be gained. These screeners can ascertain a child's ability to meet cognitive and physical milestones at an early age, particularly in Prep.

If deficits are identified during these screeners, it is expected practice that written reports be provided to the parents and the school. These are interpreted by the school staff who then guide the parents through the interventions that the school may provide and explain which interventions may be necessary through other medical or para-medical experts. These expert interventions may include speech therapy, having a child's hearing or vision tested more thoroughly, or initial cognitive assessments to ensure that the child is progressing as expected.

Again, please welcome and embrace any intervention that teachers may provide. It is only one part of the very complex jigsaw puzzle that makes up your child. I do offer a word of caution: every person will have some deficits and OTs could recommend interventions for most of the population.

The extent to which a child has been exposed to life experiences will give them the ability to perform well on some elements of the screeners. While the written report narrative may indicate deficits, please explain the wider story so that the OTs and teachers understand the context in which your child may have performed on a particular screener. If you are aware of a legitimate deficit, understand the report and follow through any recommended interventions, your child will benefit greatly.

As an experienced teacher, I understand that news indicating your child's reduced ability to learn at the pace of others may come as an unsettling surprise. Please be assured that the teachers are going to walk the journey with you. We give you the news because we want what is best for your child and intend to help them.

It is normal for parents to be reluctant to face the reality that their child may need some extra assistance. The reality is that some children need more medical or learning intervention than others. It is not always possible for schools to provide every intervention, and it is common for teachers to call in experts to provide specialist intervention.

Other School Personnel

There are various other adults whom you and your child will meet in the broader school community. At religious schools you will meet chaplains, priests or parish pastoral workers. At every primary school you will meet the crossing supervisor, a key adult with whom your child will develop a positive relationship. Crossing supervisors are parents, grandparents and other well-meaning adults who ensure the safe passage of children and adults across often busy roads. I ask you to encourage your children to follow the instructions of the crossing supervisor. I also ask you to be a good example when you are crossing the road under the crossing supervisor's instructions. Unfortunately, I have seen cases where parents have disregarded crossing supervisors. Their children learn the lesson that the crossing supervisor is not highly valued or to be taken seriously.

As a young principal, I enrolled a boy who had a level of hearing impairment. During the enrolment interview, I asked his mother about her hopes and dreams for her son at our school. Her response was that she simply wanted him to make friends. Upon our first review of his progress, I asked her how he was tracking making friends. She was very pleased that he was socially accepted and fitting into the school beautifully. I asked her again about her aspirations for her son. She again replied that she wanted him to make friends. I said, 'Good, we've achieved that goal. Let's move forward with new some academic and behavioural goals.'

This story serves as an indication of how parents need to trust school staff and how school staff need to work with parents to ensure that we achieve the right outcomes for children socially, academically and behaviourally.

LESSONS LEARNED

Parents Please:

Build rapport with all relevant school staff in your child's life

Work cooperatively with your child's teachers to establish initial goals

Communicate with your child's teacher about anything that may affect your child's education, socialisation and ability to concentrate at school

Teachers Please:

Communicate with the parents of your students as necessary

Ask multiple questions of parents to identify the needs of their children

Communicate with specialists and experts to gain understanding of children's needs where required

4 Enquiries at School

There are many times when you will need to engage with your child's school. Sometimes you will need to understand the context of a school decision. At other times you may want to share information about your child. Of course, there may be times when you aren't happy with something that has allegedly happened at school. How and when you engage will either build or erode a culture of trust and collaboration.

We will unpack how parents and teachers can engage to build a positive culture and constructive patterns of enquiry.

Questions Parents Should Ask Teachers

If a parent has a query about something that has happened in the classroom or in the school, their first port of call will likely be their child's teacher. The questions that parents and teachers ask each other should develop a culture of enquiry, collaboration and trust. When a child comes home and expresses concern about something that has happened at school, the parent has a variety of response options. A parent who believes the child's recount of events may demand answers from the teacher. Another parent may develop a culture of enquiry, trust and collaboration by asking the teacher some very simple but relevant questions:

'What happened regarding the alleged incident?'

'What is the school's policy on such-and-such a matter?'

'This is what my child has reported. Could you give me your account of what happened so I can fully understand the situation?'

'This is my child's point of view. What is the school's position or what do the other children report, so I can fully appreciate what happened?'

These questions encourage a pattern through which school, teacher and parents can work together for the benefit of the child. If a parent calls with an accusatory tone, writes an aggressive email or appears at the school and demands that the teacher respond to allegations, the teacher should stay composed and ask constructive questions to strengthen the relationship.

If the child knows that their parents, their teachers and the school's leadership team are working together for their benefit, then they can't play school off against home or vice versa.

Respectful questions allow each party to hear the other's account of what happened. This method encourages the child to tell the truth so that the situation can be resolved and education can continue harmoniously and collaboratively.

When a parent wants to respond to a child's concerns, their response to the child should include a commitment to follow up with the school on the issue. They should believe their child's story initially, with the caveat that they will seek further information from the school. They should listen carefully and ask questions to clarify what happened. If a child comes home after school and presents an allegation, their parents must discern the best course of action in response. (Note that I am using the word 'allegation', as at this stage all we have is the child's recollection of events.) The parents could immediately contact the teacher to arrange a discussion at a mutually convenient time or send off an emotive email quoting the child verbatim, accusing the school or somebody else of whatever the child says happened.

Alternatively, they may choose to sleep on it and digest the story. They now have the opportunity to think through the best way to respond. This may involve arranging a time to discuss with the child's teacher, perhaps through a quick pop-in the next morning. Whichever method of communication the parent chooses to take, I encourage them to use those questions provided above to create a culture of enquiry, collaboration and trust. This offers the teacher the opportunity to respond and put forward their recollection of events. It also gives them time to gather information if needed.

It's not uncommon for parents to demand that the school respond immediately with action against any children who might have done wrong by their child. This presents a dilemma for teachers, whose response to other children is not the concern of the complaining child or parents. Understandably, parents want reassurance that the situation is being handled in the best interests of all concerned. Parents and teacher can work together through calm attention, listening and exploration.

Why Parents Engage with School Staff

When a parent goes to their child's school, they usually approach the teachers or the principal for one of four reasons. After a parent has expressed their issue, the teacher or other staff member should ask what the parent needs from them. Once that question is asked, parents can reflect on why they have gone to the school. I'm now going to explain the four reasons why parents go to talk to schools: **venting, seeking information, making suggestions and seeking solutions.**

If they come to vent, they might want to express their disappointment at their child's progress or attitude. They know the school staff are doing all they can, but they just have to say something about it. They then walk away satisfied and ready to continue the tough educational journey with their child.

If they're coming to seek information, it might be a question of how long an exam regime or monitoring system has been in place to track their child's progress. In this case, they are simply wanting to know the history of the current practice or protocol.

Parents make a suggestion if their child is not performing to expectation, or if they are having difficulty understanding how their child is tracking. They may ask the school for regular information about the Australian Curriculum so that they can monitor and support the teacher's endeavours in teaching their child. They're offering a suggestion to support the school.

Finally, parents seeking a solution may ask what the teacher will do to support their child's learning development, and what they as parents can do to help the teacher support their child.

I would encourage teachers and principals to ask themselves what a parent needs when they come in to have a conversation. Once the parent can articulate what they need, then the teacher or principal can tailor their response to meet that need with an understanding of the context. It's not always easy but it's worth the journey.

Response to Needs

Let's turn our attention to how teachers might create a culture of trust, collaboration and enquiry when responding to a parent's concerns or questions. A teacher fielding aggressive, angry or confused parents may feel defensive and respond in a way that is less than welcoming. Teachers need to step back, breathe, thank the parents for their enquiry and calmly proceed to listen. The teacher's response may depend upon the style and delivery of the question.

If the parent demands an immediate response, the teacher may be wise to listen to their point of view. The teacher should plan on asking one or two simple yet probing questions of genuine enquiry. **'What are your needs right now?'** is the first question. This shows the parents that they have been listened to and that the teacher will work with them.

The parent may have concrete needs: time, information, better communication from the school. They may also have symbolic or deep needs, which I will explain shortly.

If the teacher asks the question about the parent's needs, a supplementary question could be **'What would that look like?'** or **'How do you imagine that to work in a school environment?'**. This puts the onus on the parents to work with the teacher to solve the problem. The questions **'What are your needs right now?'**, **'What would that look like?'** and **'What and how will that work in a school environment?'** indicate to parents that the teacher is listening and prepared to create options for improvement. The simple question about needs encourages the parent to stop and think. It can also take emotion out of the situation, allowing parent and teacher to work together.

Behavioural scientist and negotiator Allan Parker identifies three needs: material / concrete, symbolic and deep (Parker, 2019). Material or concrete needs are those things in life that are tangible and measurable: time, food, shelter, clothing, money and possessions. The concrete needs of a parent may include communication, time, information and resources to support their child's learning. When a teacher asks a parent about their needs, they should pay attention to the category in which the parent's response falls. Once this is identified, planning should be relatively straightforward.

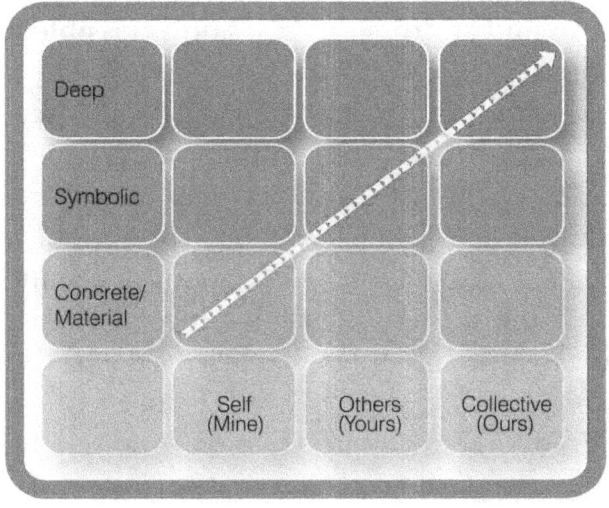

The symbolic needs of parents include the recognition of their child through affirmations. Parents also like to be recognised for the effort they are making to support their child's education. This can be as simple as the teacher acknowledging the commitment they have shown in assisting their child to meet school obligations.

When it comes to deep needs, parents may be seeking the trust of the teachers in their belief that they are fulfilling their parenting obligations. Parents may also seek a strong professional relationship with the school.

Teachers also have needs. Of course, we don't expect parents to concern themselves with these. In the event of a facilitated conversation between parents and teachers, the question can be asked of both parties. Once goals are aligned, then planning for the child's education and welfare is sequential.

The third element in this analysis is the needs of the child. It is the collective responsibility of parents and teachers to determine what the child requires to get a good education. Children need material resources to make learning possible. They need time and space to learn. They need guidance, skills and knowledge. They need explicit instruction around new topics. They need opportunities to collaborate, explore, discover, learn, succeed, fail and try again. They need feedback indicating successes and ways to improve. Children need all these things provided by their parents and their teachers. Rarely will children express their needs eloquently in primary school. It is the responsibility of their advocates to ensure that these are planned for and addressed. This is only possible in a culture of trust, collaboration and enquiry.

Generally speaking, the question 'What are your needs?' rarely needs to be asked formally, as there is a common understanding of needs at school and at home. At the point of enrolment, the interviewer may ask the parents what they hope the school will provide for their child. Parents sometimes ask about the school's expectations of them. If the parents wish to proceed with the enrolment, it is safe to assume that the needs align and that both parties agree to their obligations.

The needs of children, parents and teachers are relatively self-explanatory. Parents want their children to be happy and safe and to get a good education. They want open, honest and regular communication from the school. Teachers want trust, communication and support from the parents.

Unhealthy Models of Parenting

There are a few parenting types that may hinder the goal of healthy communication. These include the helicopter parents who hover over their child's schooling and social engagements. They usually communicate with the school on every little matter. Helicopter parents may not even be conscious of their constant presence in their child's life.

Then there are the lawnmower parents. These parents clear the path and smooth the way for their child. They eliminate any bumps in the road that their child may tread. Like helicopter parents, lawnmower parents are well-meaning. But while they may be minimising their child's pain, they are not doing them any favours.

Environment for Learning

Education expert John Hattie believes that the biggest factor in a child's learning is the child itself. Hattie has identified the factors that most affect a child's learning. The most influential people are the child and their teachers (Hattie, 2009). The needs of the child and the teachers should be met to create an environment where learning can be maximised. It is the mutual responsibility of parents and teachers to create this environment.

What does such an environment look like? Parents want what is fair for their children. Some parents may believe that all children should receive the same time and resources. I agree that all should get the same learning opportunities, but this does not extend to time and resources. As explained by leading American special needs educator Richard Lavoie, fairness is about giving children what they need (Lavoie). If someone were to stop breathing, they would be given CPR. Only they would get the required treatment. That is fair because they have that need; not everyone present would receive CPR, which would be irresponsible and dangerous. Not everyone gets the same and that's fair, as long as their needs are being met.

Not all children will get the same attention in class. Not all children need the same attention to learn. Some children are highly motivated self-directed learners. Others require individualised attention to guide and monitor their learning journey. Some children grasp concepts after the first instruction, while other children take longer via multiple methods of instruction. All children require specific feedback, and this too will vary according to the child's needs.

Homework

Primary school children will need the guidance of their parents to fulfil homework obligations. Homework is an emotive topic and can be a source of great stress for children and their families. Regardless of personal opinions, I would encourage parents to support the school. Homework has caused great debate in my own home, so I offer some ideas to navigate through its joys and challenges. Firstly, the exception to the definition of homework is reading. Daily engagement with books and reading should take place from a child's earliest years and not be considered a homework task. Reading should be a mandatory exercise. Primary school educators and authors agree that it sets children up for life.

In the early years of primary school, homework is likely to consist of children practising sight words and basic facts like simple arithmetic. Older children may be asked to write sentences, practise spelling words and harder mental arithmetic, and possibly do some project work. For children to fulfil these expectations, they need dedicated time and a supervised space conducive to doing homework. Acknowledging that families and children lead busy lives, teachers often set homework that is due after a few days or a week.

Parents, you are asked to not to do your children's homework. It must be their own work.

Teachers are reminded not to set any previously untaught work as homework. Homework is designed to reinforce concepts and should not require parents to 'teach' new topics. It is designed to give children good study habits for secondary school and beyond.

Homework has minimal impact on improving primary school children's learning achievements. There is a model that was in vogue a few years ago called the Homework Grid, developed by educator Ian Lillico (Lillico, 2004). This model promotes a range of educational and academic activities, along with life skills and tasks. These tasks often require parents to engage with their children. Homework is a good way for parents to be involved in their children's learning journey. Hopefully stress levels can be minimised. If homework causes stress, then discuss models of learning with your child's teacher.

Children's Social Network

Another critical way to support your child's learning is to know their social networks. Know who their friends are and discuss what happened during their school day. This will help you understand and support their social development. School is about academics, but it's also about working in a social environment. A child who feels safe in their social networks will be present to learn. As children develop social networks, parents can foster and encourage friendships by facilitating play dates. This also helps parents to build their social network with the parents of their children's friends. These people are important for you and your children, as they will reciprocate support when needed.

Let's work together to create physical and cultural spaces that maximise learning.

Teaching Beyond the Three Rs

Together we will teach them English, maths and other academic subjects. We will also teach them about life, health, problem-solving and how to cultivate the good manners and qualities we hope they retain for life. Let's explore some of the more sensitive areas of educating the whole person.

During what have traditionally been called sex education classes, the anatomically correct names for body parts will be used. This is confronting for some parents. Most teachers will prepare families by informing them of what is going to be taught.

This allows parents to brief their children. My experience indicates that some families will find sex ed too confronting and believe it to be outside the responsibility of teachers. These parents may request that their child be withdrawn from such classes, with the intent to educate them when they believe they are most ready for such information. This presents a dilemma for teachers because a child who has been withdrawn stands out from the crowd and may lag behind their peers. It is right for parents to be aware of what is being taught, working together with teachers to ensure that a consistent message is delivered.

Teaching about body parts, relationships and sex education is a challenge for most teachers. However, this material forms part of the Australian Curriculum and teachers must endeavour to present it in an informative and precise manner. Often relationship 'experts' may be brought in to teach particularly sensitive material. These people will have more experience than teachers in addressing relationships, personal development, bodily changes and similar topics. Although some parents may prefer to do this education themselves, children may feel more comfortable sitting with their peers and discussing the topics. It's not uncommon for schools to run parent–child nights where children are with their mates but in the company of their parents. During the evening it is a common strategy for the presenter to ask questions inviting parents and children to engage in conversation. This is a successful strategy whereby children and parents work in conjunction with the school to discuss sensitive material.

While some parents would like to believe that their children haven't been exposed to topics of a sexual nature, my experience would suggest that they are often exposed through television and social media before parents are ready for such experiences.

> *There was one such occasion where a seven-year-old boy was discussing with his classmates some very sexually explicit material. When this was explained to his mother, she didn't believe it possible that he had knowledge of such concepts because he was very limited in his access*

to television shows and social media. Upon further investigation it became apparent that the boy had seen an advertisement for a current affairs program discussing a very adult topic of a sexual nature while he was watching a family-friendly television show. He then shared that story with classmates. The news got back to families and the principal had to investigate. To her credit, the mother visited the principal to explain the context of her son's learning and apologise for not believing exposure to such topics possible in a relatively protected household.

Although families make every effort to protect their children, exposure is sometimes unavoidable and it is often better to educate children sooner rather than later.

Similarly, some parents might prefer to educate their children about diet or the use of drugs. These topics are part of the Australian Curriculum, and teachers have a responsibility and obligation to present such material. Health-related topics can present a challenge for teachers. When they accept that children's families may have different opinions, they may face a dilemma: should the school impose its own moral and ethical stance around what constitutes a healthy diet (even if based on the Australian Curriculum)? How can teachers avoid promoting their own philosophy about the use of drugs? Can a teacher present the material in an objective way? Teachers need to be very cautious about presenting any personal bias when delivering such material to impressionable children who will, of course, go home and quote what they have been taught.

Healthy Living

There is an abundance of research and press around what constitutes a healthy diet for young children. Although Australian culture promotes healthy living, we also have a high obesity rate among young children (Australian Bureau of Statistics, 2018). It is usually the responsibility of parents to provide lunch for their children, while it is the responsibility of the school to provide food at canteens or tuckshops. Taking advantage of a school canteen or tuckshop is a parent's choice. While schools endeavour to provide healthy options, parents should choose the food for their children. Tuckshop food is colour-coded: red indicates that it should be avoided, orange that it should be eaten sparingly, and green that it is healthy. If the tuckshop is used as a treat, an unhealthy option every so often will cause no harm. It may even help the child make healthy choices as they learn what is available and how much they should eat.

It is a parent's responsibility to monitor their child's diet. This does not mean eliminating all unhealthy foods, but it does mean monitoring their intake of all foods. Children with minimal exposure to unhealthy foods may not know how to cope when exposed to these foods.

The daughter of a friend who only eats healthy food goes quite silly when she attends the birthday parties of friends where the usual traditional party food is available for consumption. Being rarely allowed to eat such food, she loses her good manners and gorges herself. All foods in moderation and children will be fine. Children need to be able to make sensible choices in their diet as they grow up. Restricting children from all unhealthy foods limits their ability to choose, and subsequent exposure to foods with which they are unfamiliar may present a challenge.

Santa Claus, Easter Bunny and Friends

Another philosophical debate for primary school teachers is how to share myths that engage children in their learning and life experiences. What to do when it comes time to celebrate significant events such as Easter and Christmas? Children often concentrate on the Easter Bunny and Santa Claus, who they naturally wish to believe are real.

Why does it matter that teachers and parents share an understanding of how and when a child may or may not learn that these are just stories? It is because there are occasions when the school will celebrate Easter and Christmas, and teachers may wish to engage with experiences highlighting the Easter Bunny or Santa Claus.

On such occasions, it's important for teachers to expect that children truly believe the Easter Bunny or Santa Claus is coming. However, there are occasions where more experienced and worldly children, especially those with older siblings, may in fact know that these are fictional characters. There may even be occasions when teachers ill-advisedly reveal the truth to children, hence dispelling their beliefs. It can be absolutely shattering for a child to go home and reveal that their teacher said the Easter Bunny or Santa Claus wasn't real. As a result, parents need to go into damage control. Sometimes parents have approached teachers and asked them to justify why they dispelled the childhood belief in special characters.

From personal experience, my wife and I decided how and when we would tell our children that the Easter Bunny and Santa Claus weren't real. When our son enrolled in a boys' college in Brisbane, we understood that he would be mixing with students who, under the influence of older brothers, would already know the truth. So we decided to tell him quietly at home. We asked him to see if he could really believe that these characters achieved what they allegedly did, all within 24 hours. Our son concluded that the characters probably weren't real, but instead a good story to celebrate a very important message.

The following Easter we were driving to Grandma's house with our son and his little sister sitting in the back seat. The children spotted an Easter Bunny walking down the street. Our daughter was filled with excitement and expressed delight by saying, 'Isn't it great that the Easter Bunny is here!' Thankfully our son played along, giving his  parents a wink. Once our daughter enrolled in a girls' college, we followed the same procedure and asked her to think through the stories.

In Christian schools, the Christ story is an important part of a child's education. Teachers are usually very skilled at weaving in the special story of Santa Claus with the Christ story. Similarly, the significance of new life and the symbols that we celebrate at Easter can be interwoven with the story of the Easter Bunny. There is nothing more delightful than the joy on a child's face when they see the footprints of the Easter Bunny outside the classroom, or the Christmas tree with gifts under it. There is also nothing more devastating than when a teacher shatters a belief in these special characters. Teachers should commit to letting children believe in the wonders of Christmas and Easter. If a teacher dispels the myths that a child holds dear in their heart, parents may wish to adopt those questions that we have discussed earlier. 'What is the school's policy on telling the children about Santa and the Easter Bunny? Can you help me understand why this was said and done?' is a constructive approach. Teachers need to be sensitive to the beliefs that children hold sacred.

The Tooth Fairy is another example: children firmly believe that they will be visited overnight by a small fairy who will replace the tooth or teeth hidden under their pillow with money. The loss of baby teeth happens frequently in primary schools, so teachers are usually the recipients of this exciting news. Again, it is not the place of a teacher to dispel the story. As children grow older, they will understand that the Tooth Fairy is probably their parents replacing the tooth with a gold coin (and with the cost inflation we should stick to gold coins and nothing more!). Parents are encouraged to be realistic about what a tooth is worth when reimbursing their child. Is a tooth worth a gold coin or $20? (See Chapter 6 for the value of rewards.)

In simple terms, I believe it is wise to educate your children as soon as you believe they'll be mixing with peers who already know the reality of these characters. It can be embarrassing or disappointing if a child has heartfelt beliefs crushed by a peer who laughs at them, or by a teacher who inadvertently says, 'Don't you know it's just a story?' There may be no intent involved, but the emotional reaction from a child will be very real when they realise that their beliefs are changing as they get older. It will also be a milestone that their parents have to accept.

Australian comedian Kitty Flanagan was criticised in late 2014 for saying on the television show The Project that Santa wasn't real (Molloy, 2014). Some viewers were distressed because their young children had been watching the show and were stunned at what they heard. How could the parents have responded? In Kitty's own words: they could have told their children that she was an idiot, and how would she know? Put more diplomatically, parents were left with damage control!

Children may learn the realities of life before their parents are ready. So be prepared, parents—that is the lesson.

In closing this chapter, I advise parents to be positive about education. Primary schools set the foundations for future learning. Parents and teachers must work together in a culture of trust, collaboration and enquiry.

Here is a model that I have created to illustrate trust.

Trust Model

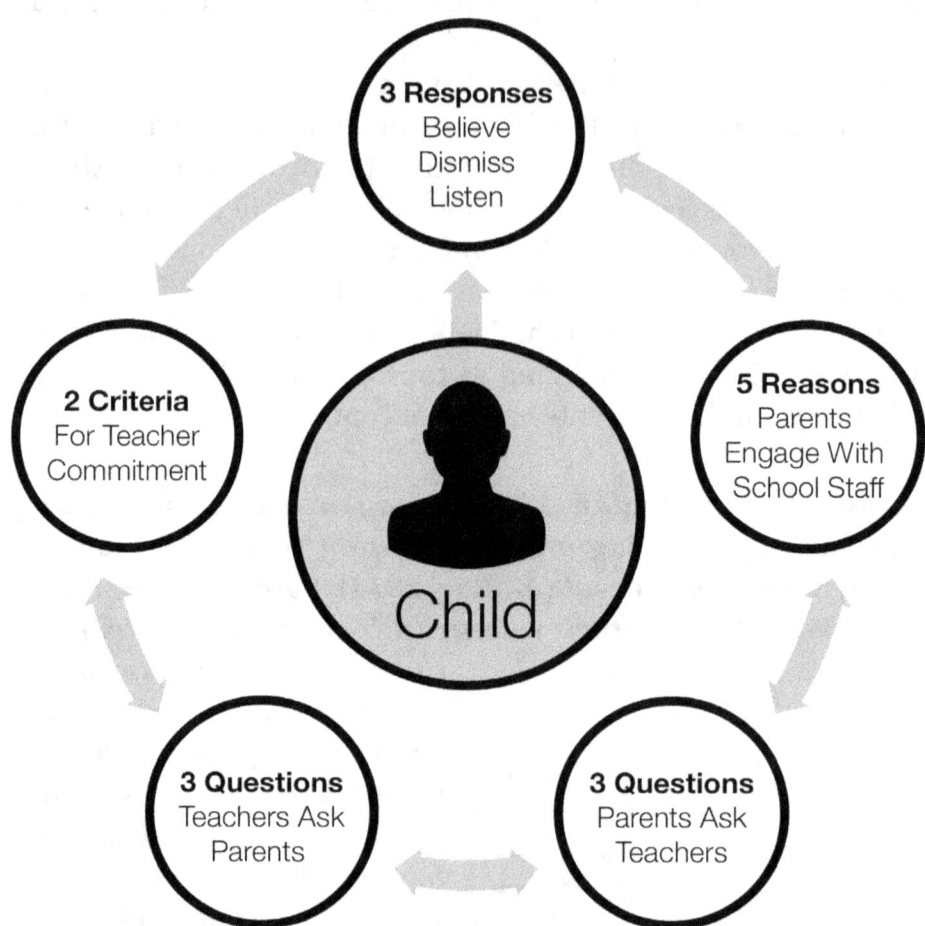

3 Parental Responses to Child's Account
- Believe without question: risk of dismissing others' truth (child may not be perfect)
- Dismiss: risk of missing something important (child could have legitimate issue)
- Listen cautiously and commit to following up with the school (preferred response). There are always two sides to the story!

5 Reasons Why Parents Engage With School Staff
- Vent about a problem
- Seek context to understand rationale for school matter
- Seek a solution: parents may want a problem solved
  Seek advice: parents may want advice on how to fix an issue
- Offer a solution: parents may have expertise that can solve a school problem

3 Questions Parents Should Ask Teachers
- What happened at school today? (My child gave their recount, so I seek the school's story)
- What is the school's policy or protocol on this matter? (Staff explain school's practice)
- What can we collectively do to support my child's education? (Working together)

3 Questions Teachers Should Ask Parents
- What do you need? (Tries to meet the needs of the parents and values their input)
- What do you think that would look like in my class or school? (Invites parent to reflect on possible realities)
- Anything else I can do? (Invites the parent to raise any issues before closing)

2 Criteria for Teacher Response to a Parent Request
- Is the request realistic? (Can the teacher fulfil the request?)
- Is the request sustainable? (Can the teacher repeat and maintain the action?)

LESSONS LEARNED

Parents Please:

Ask questions of enquiry

Let school staff resolve school matters at school

Teachers Please:

Keep parents informed about sensitive topics to be discussed at school

Be prepared to teach the sensitive topics of the curriculum with confidence and knowledge

Ask parents what they need and what their child needs

5 Transitions and Milestones

Children will celebrate personal milestones at school. They will also experience transitions when starting school and when moving schools. Such milestones and transitions should be celebrated or at least acknowledged. Children need to be prepared by their parents and teachers. This will minimise stress and maximise the value of the experience. How and when families and schools celebrate transitions and milestones may prompt discussion. Here are some guidelines for such acknowledgements.

As a child moves through their young life, there will be many rites of passage: ceremonies or rituals that occur when an individual leaves one group to enter another. These transitions often involve a significant change of status in society or within the individual's group. Rites of passage for primary school children include birthdays, changing year levels, moving schools and celebrating sacraments. Parents and school staff have a role to play in guiding and supporting children as they move through each of these transitions.

Let's look at some of the transitions particularly related to school: as children move from kindergarten to Prep, there will be a significant change. There is then a transition to mark the end of each school year. As children exit primary school there will be another significant transition from a safe environment where they are the 'biggest fish in the pond' to one where they are the 'smallest fish in the sea'. In Christian schools, children will also experience a sacramental program. Significant rites of passage carry increased responsibilities, which we'll explore later. Let's see how we can support a child through these transitions.

Smoothing Transitions

There are mechanisms that will help children and parents thrive through the transition of moving into and through school.

As a child moves from kindergarten to Prep, a degree of preparation is required of parents and school staff. The child could be preferred (not expected) to have certain skills: independence, life skills, language development and fine and gross motor skills. Some schools have introduced Prep-readiness programs to support families preparing their children for the learning that lies ahead. It is critical that children be as familiar with school as possible. Schools will usually provide opportunities for parents and children to visit and familiarise themselves with the environment.

A tip for parents and teachers: avoid calling Prep children 'preppies'. It infantilises them. They are now school students, ready to learn.

My observations indicate that children are coming to school with fewer social and life skills than in previous years. Many are now starting school at a younger age, which may contribute to their underdeveloped skills. These deficits include:
- Delayed speech development or unclear speech
- Inability to recognise their name or letters in their name
- Little interest in stories and nursery rhymes
- Attention difficulties e.g. difficulty staying on task

- Basic concepts: under, over, right, left, next to, in the corner of
- Eating difficulties
- Sensory-seeking or sensory-avoiding behaviours
- Inability to track with eyes
- Lack of interest in drawing and colouring-in
- Inability to hold a pencil or glue stick
- Difficulty sitting still on a chair
- Clumsiness or falling over
- Doesn't, can't or won't follow instructions
- Socialisation problems: separation concerns or inability to play with peers
- Limited persistence and resilience
- Fatigues quickly.

Let's explore what school staff and parents can do to prepare children for Prep and the numerous transitions that will occur thereafter.

A mother called me and said, 'Andrew, what's happening about my son's placement for next year?' I reassured her about the process: there would be a cross-section of children spread across the three learning groups for the following year. They would have experienced teachers, and her son would be in a class with some of his friends. At the conclusion of this conversation the mother said, 'I trust the teachers and I trust your decision-making process.' I asked her what she was worried about and she said, 'Actually, I don't know. I just need to be reassured.' After a five-minute conversation she left content that she had been informed, that her trust in the staff was well-founded, and that her son

would be looked after the following year. The message for teachers and principals on this occasion is: share accurate information and reassure parents to create a culture of trust, collaboration and enquiry. The child will be the beneficiary of positive relationships between home and school.

Eldest or Only Child Entering School

The prospect of handing over your eldest or only child to teachers can be quite daunting. On such occasions, it's not uncommon for parents to ask many questions about the process of children being assigned to classes. Teachers should explain the process and enable parents to trust the school to make decisions in the best interests of their child.

Twins Entering School

The placement of twins is a unique situation. Kindergarten teachers should advise the parents and the school of the best solution for the children. Placing twins in the same Prep class can give them a familiar face to learn with in the classroom, and a degree of comfort in their first year of formal schooling. The kindergarten teacher may determine that children should be separated, particularly if they have strong personalities or if one is more dominant than the other. Twin placement should be determined on a case-by-case basis.

> *A mother and father approached me to advise them on the merits of placing their twins in the same Prep class. I asked, 'What does the kindergarten teacher say?' The kindergarten teacher had recommended that the children be separated in their first year of schooling because they had strong personalities and were competitive with each other. Separation would allow them to develop as individuals and become independent people. I advised the*

mother to listen to the kindergarten teacher's advice and promised to share observations from my own staff during the orientation process. The mother was then quick to suggest that she ask the twin girls for their opinion. As the girls were only four-and-a-half years old, I immediately advised that young children don't have any input into their own educational placement. The decision must rest with the teachers and leadership team with advice from the kindergarten teacher and the parents. It became apparent that the mother had a degree of anxiety about her only children entering school. I asked her: was this about her children or her anxiety? She freely admitted that a degree of anxiety was clouding her decision-making processes. Once she was reassured that our decisions would be in the best interests of her children, she felt comfortable and trusted us with the placement process. She was also pleased that our staff would consult the kindergarten teacher and use orientation observations, transition documents and other relevant information to determine the best place for

her twins. This process of consultation and discernment takes place at the end of every year. If twins are not separated in Prep, they can easily be separated in Grade One or Grade Two as they develop their own personalities and the teachers get to know them.

Important Micro Life Skills: Making the Path Easier

If your child will be wearing a uniform, have them try it on in the days leading up to starting school. They should be able to independently manage everything they will be using. These skills free up teachers and give children a sense of responsibility and purpose. The sooner parents start to train and support their children, the better the outcomes.

As they continue through primary school, children will grow and reach more physical milestones, most notably losing teeth and possibly reaching puberty. Parents may choose to inform teachers when these things are happening so they are aware that the child may be distracted at school and continue to support them.

Language Skills

Another skill that is important for a child's development is the use of language, both receptive (listening and comprehending) and expressive (speaking and expressing themselves). It is important that parents and school staff monitor a child's language development very early on in their schooling.

As children become more confident with the use of language, they should begin to recognise their own written name. They will recognise and pronounce letters of the alphabet, and then common words associated with life skills: on / off, hot / cold, stop / go. These words will become part of the vernacular that places their language development in a real-life context.

Social Skills, Positive Interactions and Early Relationship Skills

Social skills include sharing, taking turns and listening. Children will be expected to respond to many adults in primary school. They will have their classroom teacher and possibly a school officer. They will have specialist teachers and a teacher librarian. Children will also develop a broad social network. They should be encouraged to mix socially with children of a similar age. For only children who live in an adult world, I would encourage parents to seek out other families for peer engagement before school starts or at the earliest opportunity within the school environment.

Visit your child's school before they begin Prep. Many schools have play dates after orientation sessions so that the children become familiar with their environment. This will give them a sense of ownership on their first day.

Schools have become astute at assisting teachers and parents to get children ready through Prep-readiness programs. One model looks like this: the children who are entering Prep the following year are invited, along with their parents, to visit the school for three consecutive Wednesday mornings. They will engage in Prep activities under the guidance of early-years teachers and school officers or volunteer parents.  This gives the children an exposure to the learning environment of a Prep classroom.

While the children are engaged in the classroom, a member of the leadership team and another early-years teacher will give the parents guidance around the four topics already discussed: language development, independence skills, social skills and motor skills. The school staff will explain how parents can prepare their children by practising these skills at home.

A key message of the Prep-readiness program is that all children are on different learning journeys and will progress at individual rates. The program also promotes a culture of trust, collaboration and enquiry: parents ask questions while school staff share their knowledge and invite comment from more experienced parents.

As a child moves from grade to grade in primary school, their responsibilities increase. Upon starting school, they may have the responsibility of looking after their own bag. When they move up a grade, the responsibility will evolve: they may have to go to the drop-off and pick-up line at the end of the school day. As children become teenagers, they are probably going to have a phone and corresponding responsibilities. These transitions are rites of passage, and children need to be supported during the process.

I have watched parents carry their children's school bags to and from classrooms. When I approach the parents, I enquire whether the child is sick or injured. 'No, why do you ask?' is the usual response. I then ask why the child isn't carrying their own bag. At a loss for a reasonable explanation, parents often hand the child their bag. Since I have shared this message publicly within my school community, parents are more reluctant to carry their child's bag and children are more reluctant to hand their bag to their parents. The worst example I have seen was a pregnant mother carrying three school bags to her car while three children happily walked alongside her. Let children carry their own bags. I have never carried either of my children's bags to or from school. Allowing children to pack their own bags encourages confidence and independence. They will also be responsible and very capable when it comes to packing bags for family holidays.

Birthdays

Birthdays are some of the most important personal milestones that children will experience at primary school. Parents are often faced with a dilemma when deciding how to celebrate their child's birthday. Do we invite every class member? Do we invite both boys and girls? Do we invite our child's teacher? Do we invite the school officers? Do we have to follow what everyone else has done? Do we have to 'compete with the Joneses'? How much should we spend? What's the protocol on issuing invitations? All these questions are particularly pertinent during the school term.

Should invitations be distributed at school? School is certainly most convenient. If distribution can be done naturally and your child can be subtle and positive, then go for it. The distribution of invitations at school emotionally affects the birthday child, the children receiving an invitation and the children not receiving an invitation. For this reason, school staff often oversee the distribution process. Although it is not a big deal, you should be conscious of it when planning your child's birthday party.

When planning a party, evaluate the time and money that you can afford to spend. Consider how many children you wish to invite and whether you will hold the party at your house. Additional supervision may be necessary. Do some families prefer their children to only eat healthy food? Is there a limit on the value of gifts that children may be giving? All these questions require confident, clear decisions from parents. Let me give you some tips on how to walk this minefield.

Firstly, there is no obligation to have a birthday party every year for every child. This may be unrealistic and financially impossible. Secondly, there is no obligation to invite every classmate to your child's birthday party. A birthday party for a class of 30 children may be impossible and is unwise to attempt just to prevent anyone feeling left out.

One rule of thumb might be to invite the same number of children that your child is turning in years. For example, if a child is turning six, invite six friends. Children will not be included in everything and are not friends with everybody. They will understand that they don't get invited to everyone's birthday party. Invite real friends, the names you hear your child mention.

Another tip is to invite some trusted parents to assist. Adult supervision will ensure that the party stays on track. However, please don't talk among yourselves about school and teachers unless it's in a positive tone. While you're having an adult conversation around children, be very selective about what you're talking about and to whom you are talking.

Religious Milestones

A rite of passage relevant in Christian (especially Catholic) schools is the celebration of the sacraments. As children celebrate each of the sacraments (reconciliation or confession; confirmation; First Eucharist or First Holy Communion), they can begin to take on more responsibilities within their faith community and even at school. Once a child has made their First Holy Communion, they could become an altar server for parish masses and school celebrations. As they become ready for secondary school, they may be ready to join youth groups in the parish. These rites of passage associated with faith-based groups are significant. There are other parish ministries, such as reader or lector, that children may join as they get older.

New Year, New Teachers

As the end of the year approaches, children are put into the learning groups that determine which class they will be in for the following year. Some principals will ask parents for their input about their child's friends or the teaching style that best suits their needs (instruction, demonstration, conversation, experimentation, following step-by-step instructions or regular debriefing and unpacking). Parents should have confidence in the teachers, who know their children in an educational setting and are well-placed to judge the social dynamics of learning groups.

Children usually get a new class teacher each year. How you respond to the news of your child's teacher will affect how your child responds. A child who has reservations will read your cues and be more optimistic than they were prior to seeing your response. If you respond with fear and concern, your child will read that cue too. As a parent, you may need to practise a positive demeanour even if you aren't feeling it. If that proves too difficult, practise your poker face so children can't read your non-verbal cues. Parents are also advised to not listen to rumours about the reputation of staff. Every child is different and the relationship they build with their teachers will vary from year to year.

Parents sometimes need reassurance from teachers while learning groups are being determined. They might be concerned about their child's class groups, support requirements, behaviour in class, academic progress or friendships. Please note that parental input into the process of assigning children to learning groups may be discouraged. The final decision rests with school staff and unfortunately all requests cannot be accommodated.

Allocating children and teachers to classes is one of the more complex tasks undertaken by school leadership teams. Each school has its own process for putting children into learning groups and releasing class lists. A typical process looks like this: teachers are instructed to split the children into the relevant number of classes for the following year. They will consider the children's social network and the academic profile and behavioural dynamics of the class groups. Teachers are instructed to assign an equitable cross-section to each learning group. They do not assign children to their colleagues. This is the domain of the leadership team, with possible input from relevant role-holders such as the support team and curriculum leaders.

Assigning Children to Groups

While this task is being done, it is possible that parents may be invited to share relevant information about their children with their current teacher. Any confidential information should be emailed to the principal, who has the final say on class groups. The principal should only change a child's class if the confidential information is relevant to the child's class or teacher, and only after consultation with the relevant teachers. The confidential information does not need to be shared with the teachers. The rationale for inviting input is that education is a collaborative process between home and school. It is also important to note that the standard line from school staff when responding to parental requests should be something like: 'Thanks for your input. We will take all information into consideration during our deliberations to assist us to make the most appropriate decision, without making any promises'.

The question of when to publish class lists is also important. Should children only be told who their teacher is, leaving parents to discover who the other students in the class are? Should lists be released at the end or the start of the year? Publishing lists at the end of the year allows children to meet their new teacher and parents to promote the opportunities ahead. The downside is that unhappy children and parents may need support in accepting a less-desired class or teacher. Early publication allows more time for engagement with the principal if necessary. Ultimately, parents need to accept class lists and assignments of teachers unless there is a glaringly obvious mistake. Occasionally teachers and principals make mistakes with child placement and teacher allocation. On these occasions, principals should listen and review decisions in the best interests of the child and the teacher.

A 'Bump Up' process will be in place to allow students to meet their new teachers and classmates. This is usually facilitated in the new classroom during the last week of the school year. The process should minimise student concerns about facing the unknown.

How you as a parent respond to class and teacher allocation will help build a culture of trust, collaboration and enquiry. I advise promoting the positive experiences that lie ahead. It is important to trust the process, support the decision and encourage the child to look forward to the following year. Enjoy the holidays and plan with optimism for the future.

Moving a child to another class is not a simple exercise. The process that staff have undertaken to assign children is a time-consuming and thoughtful one. The movement of one child may have multiple implications. It can affect the balance of sexes, the social dynamics, and the academic and behavioural profiles of two classes.

A mother approached me, concerned about a teacher who she believed would not be good for her daughter. She was basing this opinion on what she had heard from other parents about the teacher's teaching style. We had multiple meetings and I continually promoted the positive qualities of the teacher. Trusting the process, I left the child in the class as planned. At the start of Term Four in the following year, the same mother found me and apologised for questioning the decision. Her daughter was having a fantastic year. I appreciated the feedback and assured the mother that an apology, while graciously received, was unnecessary: parents need to be their children's greatest advocates and are only acting in their best interests. And remember—so are teachers!

Moving from School to School

The most dramatic school transition for a child is the move from their current school to a new school. Sometimes families relocate due to parents' work circumstances, and sometimes due to lifestyle changes. On such occasions, families often choose a school close to their new work or home. They may research which school in the local area will best meet their child's educational needs. There are families who change schools because they believe a new school will be better at meeting the educational needs of their children. As a child finishes primary school, they will prepare to move to secondary school (the exception being at P-12 schools where a child can remain from Prep to Year 12). Regardless of the reason, there is one common message: changing schools and choosing a new school are primarily parents' decisions. At best, parents may ask their child for an opinion after they have visited the school.

Choosing a School

A child's opinion is likely to be based on the facilities they see, the warmth of response from the person who welcomes and interviews them, and the school that their friends are going to attend. While the child's thoughts are important, they are often not sound reasons upon which to base an educational decision. I advise parents to consider the philosophy of the school, the academic outcomes past and present, the parental engagement, the educational opportunities, the presence of likeminded families, the school's location and proximity to home, and its associated costs.

There are some simple things you can do to make your child feel calm about the change. There should be closure from the school that the child is leaving. It is important that children have time to say goodbye to their friends and teachers. Moving to the new school and environment means time for new transitional processes. You can visit the new school and engage with orientation programs.

These transitions can be challenging for parents watching their children grow up, but are also cause for celebration. They are an opportunity for stimulation and the encouragement of emotional intelligence. Every transitional experience is a time to learn, adjust and explore new possibilities.

LESSONS LEARNED

Parents Please:

Celebrate transitions with scaled celebrations

Use each transition for new responsibilities that recognise children's growing maturity

Trust school staff with the process of assigning children to classes

Have closure at previous schools and engage with new schools

Teachers Please:

Don't call Prep students preppies

Be faithful to the school process of assigning children to classes

6 Affirmations

Every family and teacher will have their own beliefs about celebrating the achievements of children. There will be numerous opportunities for affirmation as children progress in their learning and improve their physical and artistic skills. The challenge for teachers and parents is to make each affirmation meaningful so that children treasure the acknowledgement. Parents should be aware that their expectations may not match those of teachers. It is important to transparently share rationales for affirmation.

We need to affirm children for their effort as well as their ability and behaviour. Children may be very bright and achieve good results at school or in other domains without maximum effort. We should certainly celebrate success: a child who has come first, second or third should receive suitable recognition. But a child who achieves a personal best in any area of life should be celebrated with the same degree of excitement as a child who receives a prize for excellent results. Let's reward effort. Let's reward improvement. Let's reward progress.

Some parents may believe that a child should be rewarded or acknowledged for participation. The problem is that participation awards reward children for getting out of bed and turning up. If the child shows improvement or achieves a personal best, that effort should be acknowledged. But rewarding participation alone does not send the right message.

My experience would suggest that participation ribbons become meaningless very quickly. My own children have a number of these ribbons. They lie crumpled in the bottom of a drawer and often have no recognition of the event, date, year or school. A token that acknowledges effort, on the other hand, can have a positive impact that lasts a long time.

Ownership of Work

It is right to help your children when they need it. But we can only reward a child's work and progress when we know that they have earned it through their own efforts. Teachers have many stories of parents seeing their child's results and saying, 'I worked so hard on that. Why didn't my child receive a better result?' or similar expressions of disappointment. The reason might be that the teacher knew it wasn't the student's work, and therefore not acceptable for assessment. Supervise your child, assist and guide them, provide them with resources. But it must be their work that the teachers are marking, correcting, acknowledging and celebrating.

Now that we have established who and what get rewarded, we need to explore appropriate degrees of recognition.

> *After climbing a great hill, one only finds that there are many more hills to climb.*
>
> *Nelson Mandela*

Appropriate Recognition

There are many reasons to praise children in primary school. These include good behaviour, improvement in work, service to the school community and improving social dynamics (being considerate and kind rather than reactive). We need to remember that the benchmark we establish for the first models of reward requires the following rewards to have similar quality of value. There will be numerous significant events outside school where children will be rewarded and acknowledged. Again, the value of the reward must match the occasion.

At school, recognition needs to match the achievement and occasion. In life, recognition sometimes matches the achievement and occasion but sometimes doesn't occur at all. Preparing for and handling both outcomes well is a sign of strength, character and maturity.

Primary school students are recognised for individual and group achievements. Individual rewards can be as simple as verbal praise, a pat on the back, a high-five or ticks on the child's work. If the child's behaviour deserves more significant recognition, then something longer-lasting may be worth considering. A certificate presented at a school assembly may be the recognition due. This is all about giving legitimate, positive feedback. (Feedback that leads to improvement will be discussed shortly.) Every child should receive some form of public recognition during the year. It is demoralising for children to get to the last few weeks of school without having been recognised publicly and sincerely.

If the occasion merits, the principal or a member of the leadership team may visit the classroom and acknowledge children deserving recognition. Teachers can send deserving children to visit a member of the leadership team to be praised. This process builds rapport between children and school leadership. It also demystifies the school administration setting. When children visit the school office, they should feel it is a normal part of the school and its culture. Once upon a time children only visited the office when in trouble, and in some settings that may still be the case. Even some parents get noticeably nervous when sitting in the principal's office. Their schooling must have involved some traumatic experiences leaving lasting memories! Nowadays we want children to feel safe and comfortable visiting the school office, knowing that they can sometimes expect praise, appreciation and acknowledgement.

You may have noticed that I have not suggested lollies as a reward for children at school. Teachers don't pay their students' dental bills and shouldn't be encouraging high sugar intakes, especially when diabetes and obesity are on the rise.

Fun recognition may include sticker charts, a class game or a points system leading to tangible rewards such as free time. Whatever rewards teachers negotiate with the class need to be meaningful. Often rewards may be cumulative and lead to another reward of greater value. This can apply to individual or group rewards.

If our goal is to produce children who are responsible contributors to society, then we should teach them to understand and be driven by intrinsic motivators. Children need to learn that life is not about external rewards, but about the satisfaction one should get when contributing to the greater good.

Teacher and Parent Praise

There may be occasions when teachers and parents work together to negotiate and decide on recognition and rewards. Often this collaborative approach aims to improve a child's behaviour. The hoped-for change in behaviour could be an increase in school attendance. It could be a happy transition into school on a daily basis. It could be improved engagement in class. These areas for improvement are often identified when the child is reluctant to follow school instructions and expectations. The value of the recognition should match the child's age, improvement and experiences. On such occasions, the teacher requires data rationalising why a collaborative approach may be advantageous. A collaborative approach means the child knows that their parents and teachers are working together. Yet again, we encourage collaboration for its positive flow-on effects.

With the support of guidance counsellors and other staff, teachers may work with parents to identify a specific behaviour and subsequent reward processes. Behaviours may be recorded on a daily chart that gives the child and parents feedback. The rewards must be meaningful for the child and reflect short-term goals. The occasion for reward may take place at the end of each day or each week, depending on the age of the child. The older the child, the longer the time possible between targeted behaviour and feedback.

As a parent, you may negotiate a meaningful and appropriate reward with your child. It could be money (keeping the amount minimal), a toy (of little financial value), a treat (favourite food) or a visit to somewhere of interest.

Children have been quoted as saying, 'I picked up rubbish. Do I get a reward?' No, they should not! Keeping the school clean and free from rubbish is everyone's responsibility. The reward is being proud of the environment that we create together. If teachers wish to give a reward for such behaviour, then they should make it a token that may possibly lead to greater acknowledgement. Some schools use rewards such as GETOs (Great Example to Others), which are small tokens that give recognition for a child's behaviour. These tokens then go into a weekly draw at the school assembly. The child is acknowledged by the teacher immediately for good behaviour and has the opportunity for greater recognition, without any guarantees.

Celebrations Should Match Children's Development

In primary school, major events and achievements are relatively few. Sporting success that warrants selection in representative teams deserves recognition. Academic excellence in comparison to peers across the state or nation deserves recognition. Excellence in the creative arts against a national standard deserves recognition.

In a Christian school, celebrating the sacraments is significant for families, parish and school. Graduating from primary school also deserves some acknowledgement so long as it is kept in perspective.

Graduation rituals for primary school children should be meaningful and simple. Speeches, presentation of certificates and some hospitality with refreshments are a suitable level of celebration. Gifts from the school and parents need to be kept within perspective of the age of the child and the occasion. Graduations from secondary school and university deserve greater rituals and rewards.

> *" Motivation is based on improvement, not perfection. "*
>
> Michael Grinder

I was working with a family new to my school. The two boys found school challenging, so the father promised them a motorbike if they achieved good results. A motorbike for primary school students! I suggested to the father that this reward did not match the age or experience of the children. When the daughter of a different family graduated, her parents arranged for a stretch limousine to take her and a group of friends to the end-of-year party. A stretch limousine for a 12-year-old seems just a bit out of alignment with the child's age and experience.

Carol Dweck is a professor of psychology at Stanford University and one of the world's leading researchers in the field of motivation. Her research has focused on why people succeed and how to foster success. Dweck suggests that children who put in the effort and see results will be motivated to try new things and 'have a go'. She has found that children who are naturally very bright and achieve excellent results without much effort are less likely to try new things, less likely to be risk-takers and less likely to be valuable contributors to society (Dweck, 2017). We as parents and teachers should affirm effort and work that serves the greater good.

When giving children new opportunities and experiences, allow them to fail while encouraging them to get back up again and have another go. Children are reassured when failure has minimal personal consequences. If they know they won't get hurt or embarrassed or in trouble, they are likely to persist and to try new things. If there is a fear or likelihood of physical or emotional hurt, their desire to persist diminishes. When praising effort, you should focus on strategies and new ways to refine and enhance. We want to see children stretching themselves and constantly improving. They will see that by not taking on hard things, they are not going to grow. Most children want to grow, to learn, to improve. They just need our support to do so.

On 18 August 2016, Richard Pringle's three-year-old son Hughie died suddenly following a brain haemorrhage. A year later, Richard took to social media to share what the experience had taught him. He hoped that his words would encourage other parents never to take their precious time with children for granted.

Below are the 10 lessons Richard learned after losing his son (Vonow, 2017). In his words:

1. You can never ever kiss and love too much.

2. You always have time. Stop what you're doing and play, even if it's just for a minute. Nothing's that important that it can't wait.

3. Take as many photos and record as many videos as humanly possible. One day that might be all you have.

4. Don't spend money; spend time. You think what you spend matters? It doesn't. What you do matters. Jump in puddles; go for walks. Swim in the sea, build a camp, and have fun. That's all they want. I can't remember what we bought Hughie; I can only remember what we did.

5. Sing. Sing songs together. My happiest memories are of Hughie sitting on my shoulders or sitting next to me in the car singing our favourite songs. Memories are created in music.

6. Cherish the simplest of things. Night times, bedtimes, reading stories. Dinners together. Lazy Sundays. Cherish the simplest of times. They are what I miss the most. Don't let those special times pass you by unnoticed.

7. Always kiss those you love goodbye and if you forget, go back and kiss them. You never know if it's the last time you'll get the chance.

8. Make boring things fun. Shopping trips, car journeys, walking to the shops. Be silly, tell jokes, laugh, smile and enjoy yourselves. They're only chores if you treat them like that. Life is too short not to have fun.

9. Keep a journal. Write down everything your little ones do that lights up your world. The funny things they say, the cute things they do. We only started doing this after we lost Hughie. We wanted to remember everything. Now we do it for Hettie, and we will for Hennie too. You'll have these memories written down forever and when you're older, you can look back and cherish every moment.

10. If you have your children with you. [Sic] To kiss goodnight. To have breakfast with. To walk to school. To take to university. To watch get married. You are blessed. Never ever forget that.

LESSONS LEARNED

Parents Please:

Reward effort, improvement and achievement

Keep rewards relative to the child's age and achievement

Allow children to do their own work

Cherish the simplest of things (life is too short not to have fun)

Teachers Please:

Give praise immediately and legitimately

Remember that tangible rewards are helpful (not lollies!)

Give individual and group rewards

Cherish the simplest of things (life is too short not to have fun)

7 Gifts for Children

Parents and teachers give children the gifts they need to grow, learn and become successful contributors to society. Some of the greatest gifts from a parent are time, routine, boundaries, consistency and the joy of reading. Let's explore each of these in turn.

Time

Time spent with a child is one of the greatest gifts a parent can offer. Children value and remember the time that parents spend with them. It doesn't matter what car you drive, where you spend your holidays or how much money you earn. Children will remember when Mum and Dad were at their school concert. They will remember when their parents could help with reading groups, excursions, homework, assignments and projects. As children enter the challenging times of adolescence their relationship with you will change (I am living through it right now!) but they will still want and appreciate your time, even if it is on their terms.

As our lives become busier it becomes more challenging to find moments to spend together. The time you have with your children should be quality time. It may be reading a story, doing homework together, or sitting watching television and just being together. As parents with busy working and social lives, we are investing in the futures of our children with the hours that we can spend with them. As a child becomes a teenager and faces the challenges of growing up, they know that a parent who has dedicated time to them will now be available to listen.

On a recent family holiday, I had one of the most delightful days with my children. In the morning I spent a couple of hours shopping with my daughter. This was something special to her, something she enjoyed, something she could lead. In the afternoon of the same day, I spent an hour with my son playing sport. At dinner that night I told my children what a special day it had been, and how much I had enjoyed quality time with them as individuals doing activities that meant something to them. Hopefully we will continue such simple rituals, at least until they become uncool!

Precious family time can be as little as a few minutes at the dinner table; it can be a few minutes to lie in a child's bed before they go to sleep and share a story or the events of the day; it can be the time you have while driving your children to or from school. The time you give them is critical to establishing and maintaining relationships. When they do need to have some tough conversations with you, they will know you will listen and be their greatest advocate.

It is equally important for teachers to provide their time to children. For example, a child may come to a teacher on the playground and share a story. It may be completely irrelevant to the teacher, but it means something to the child. If the teacher takes the time to listen, the child will remember that attention. Like parents, teachers must signal to children that they will be there as a compassionate listening ear when needed.

Routine

Young children appreciate knowing what's going to happen in their lives. They want to know what to expect, when to expect it, and with whom they will be engaging.

At home, children should learn the daily routine: get dressed, have breakfast, get lunch, pack school bags, go to the car and leave for school. Parents' lives become much easier when children can memorise and follow what is expected of them.

At school, teachers can establish a routine from the moment the children arrive: where do we put our bags? Where do we wait and line up? What happens when we enter the classroom? What does the teacher expect of us in class? Where do we eat lunch? What are the playground rules? What happens when the signal to return to class is sounded? All these routines give children confidence to behave within the confines of a school environment. When we teach children how to behave, we maximise learning.

Changes to school routines can be distressing for some children. These changes could include a teacher's absence, a special assembly or a gathering with other classes. Parents and teachers can minimise children's anxiety by preparing them for any anticipated changes with calm reassurance.

While routines are important, they can't be so rigid that they restrict the child from functioning. Children also need to learn to adapt and often do this better than adults. Parents and teachers should model the flexibility and resilience that children will require as they grow up.

Boundaries and Consistency

Children like to know that life has a degree of certainty about it. They also like to know that there are consequences, and that their parents and teachers have boundaries. Boundaries give children confidence that they are loved and cared for. A lack of boundaries can create a chaotic, unstructured world that presents dangerous opportunities. Children like to know that there will be consistent philosophies and behaviours practised by their parents and teachers. They appreciate knowing that their actions will draw consistent responses. However, boundaries should not be so rigid as to be constricting. Children should have unstructured downtime. They should be allowed to make their own decisions at an appropriate age, and to express themselves freely and confidently. All these things are important within the right environment.

Two highly regarded and recently retired Australian principals missed their own children's significant personal celebrations due to work commitments. Work will always be there, but your child's graduation or birthday shouldn't be missed. We all make sacrifices that we can rationalise. But the message that we send to children is that their parents had something more important than them. A word of warning: don't make a habit of missing events. Prioritise your family time.

Reading

One of the most important gifts for all children is reading. It opens up a whole new world. Start with any book and make it a paper one! Why are paper books better than reading on an iPad or similar device? They allow children to turn pages, re-read passages, look at pictures and get absorbed into a story in a way that electronic books just can't achieve. I have seen children try to swipe the front cover of a picture book. This indicates they have had minimal or no exposure to hard copy books. Give children books and encourage them into the wonderful world of reading.

From the moment a child is born until they become an independent reader, parents should show them the joy of engaging with books and literature. Babies and children enjoy worlds of words and pictures. They become interested in the characters, the plot, the imagery. Some children will find exposure to words quite challenging and may not readily engage with books. Parents and educators can model engagement with books by reading to children, having the children infer and interpret what might happen in the story, talking about the pictures and using visual cues to interpret words.

Stories have the transformative power to help children and teenagers make sense of the world. As Australian children's author Morris Gleitzman says, 'There's an absolute connection between reading good stories and all of the developments that ideally take place through childhood into adolescence' (Richardson, 2018).

It is critical that children can read and write. Early exposure to written and visual texts gives them the foundations on which they can engage with stories, and skills that they will use for the rest of their lives. Parents should feel confident to engage their children with a variety of texts. These could be picture books, comic strips, newspapers, magazines or non-fiction books. The message is simple: read to your children from an early age. Read with your children as they begin to grasp letters and words and sentences and paragraphs, and then monitor their reading as they become independent readers around the ages of seven, eight, nine and ten. Continue this involvement into their teenage years.

Children will be engaging with words in every aspect of their future career. Being able to enjoy books at a young age is a critical foundational skill. We as parents and as educators are responsible for giving them that skill.

Parents and teachers need to monitor our children's literature choices. In primary schools, books are carefully selected by teacher librarians. However, there are occasions when children may inadvertently read material that challenges their beliefs and moral positions. If this happens at school, staff should be open to parental feedback and may review the situation to determine whether the material should be kept available to children.

Finding suitable material for young boys who are reluctant readers is a challenge for parents and teachers. As boys become more independent in their reading and choice of material, they may get absorbed into either science fiction or non-fiction material such as sporting pages, music magazines and the *Guinness Book of Records*. The facts are often quite appealing, and boys may find the material engaging and easy to digest. A key factor in determining suitable literature for boys is to find material relevant to their interests that captures their attention and imagination very quickly.

Girls can also be reluctant readers. Some may find reading difficult, while others may not have identified an author or genre to their liking. This is where teacher librarians can come into their own. Teacher librarians have exceptional knowledge of literature and can offer suggestions for reluctant readers. In fact, they can offer suggestions for all readers. Girls may be drawn to series such as *Rainbow Magic* or classics like *The Chronicles of Narnia* and *Charlotte's Web*. Teacher librarians may suggest a particular author who captures girls' attention.

If you are feeling uncertain about how to guide and teach your children how to read, I encourage you to ask their primary school or kindergarten teachers about how they engage with children's stories. Books do not need to have lots of words to be very effective sources of literacy. You can ask leading questions: what do you think will happen? What does this picture tell us about the story? What does the front cover tell us? What does the title of the book tell us?

One of the great delights for parents and teachers is to see the joy on a child's face as they begin to read. As children begin to recognise letters and words, they will begin to say these sounds out loud. It is very advisable for parents to read the same book over and over again on multiple occasions. Your child will begin to predict the words and start to read from memory, pointing to words that they recognise because they are familiar with the text.

Children With Diverse or Additional Needs

Families whose children have diverse learning needs deserve special attention. These children, like all children, are gifts to their families and add to the rich tapestry of their class. Parents of a child with special needs should consider how comfortable they feel sharing their child's story with other parents and their child's classmates.

You may be wondering why it is relevant for other children or parents to know the story of a child with special needs. I would suggest that if we are building community and creating a culture of trust, collaboration and enquiry, then sharing this story allows other parents to be understanding, patient and accepting of all children in their child's class. A special needs condition could be something as simple as a medical allergy such as anaphylaxis. It could be a clinical condition such as autism spectrum disorder (ASD) or attention deficit hyperactivity disorder (ADHD), both of which are common conditions in today's classrooms.

If your child has special needs, it is critical that you share this information with the school at the point of enrolment. I also encourage you to share as much as you can with your child's class teacher. This will allow the teacher to meet the needs of the child and fully appreciate the demands placed on the family.

Some families will have tensions and struggles in accepting that their child is different or has learning needs beyond those of their average peer. Other families are quite happy to embrace their child's learning journey and to share their story to raise awareness of the condition. A popular strategy for parents is to write an open letter to the families of the child's classmates, explaining the condition and the impact it has on their child's learning, attendance at school or ability to participate in activities. This letter opens the lines of communication for all families. It also provides an opportunity for networks of practical and moral support to be established.

Sadly, not all parents are open to the diverse range of learners in every class and would prefer a homogenised group of children. However, that is not the way of the world. The diversity of children should be embraced by parents and by staff alike. Parents should talk to their own children about individual differences. We need to promote inclusive values and encourage children to look out for others.

As a parent of a child with special needs, all you may want is for your child to be included and treated like any other child. Please note that not every school can provide the resources needed by children with certain needs. Offers of enrolment to children with exceptional learning needs depend on funding models and the possibility of support from external agencies. It is important to know that the average mainstream school may not have staff with the training, qualifications or experience necessary to help children with significant needs. Despite a teacher's best intentions, it is a huge challenge to juggle the requirements of all students. Principals have an obligation to look after their staff while providing high-quality education for all students.

At the point of enrolment, I listen to parents' hopes and dreams for their child who has significant learning needs. I stress to the parents that I will only commit to a level of support that I know I can provide in terms of physical resources and additional personnel. As I have become more experienced, I am more realistic about what my school can provide. Sometimes this is enough for parents, while on other occasions they prefer other options for their child.

> *There was one family who had four children on the autism spectrum. The parents wished to enrol all their children at my school. When I considered what each child needed, I was conscious of the impact on the teachers: new challenges, additional meetings, more training and possibly more stress. I was also conscious that each child would require*

more from the teacher, hence taking time away from the other students. Could I meet the needs of all four of these children? I wasn't confident that I could. I offered a place to two of the children, not the other two siblings. Wanting all the children to be together, the family withdrew their application.

There are also numerous stories of families grateful that their children are welcomed and embraced by the school.

Parents are the greatest advocates for their children, especially children with special needs. Communication between teachers and parents is crucial for the success of a child's progress.

Managing Bullying

One of the emotional topics often discussed at school is that of bullying. Let me clarify: bullying is ongoing and persistent targeted behaviour to the detriment of one or more individuals. A fight between two peers is not bullying. A display of teasing between two peers is not bullying. That is children being naughty children, in need of discipline and consequences for their behaviours. If it is persistent, if it is targeted and if there is a power difference between the peers then it should be addressed as bullying. Some parents are very quick to use the term bullying if their child comes home and complains that a peer has done them harm. Again, let's agree on the definition: bullying needs to be repetitive and intentional.

School Camp

Children who are afforded the gifts of time, routine, boundaries and consistency will build resilience. This important trait allows children to embrace new experiences such as their first school camp. You can assist your child to build resilience for this occasion. For one thing, it would be prudent for them to have had sleepovers at a friend's house. They will become familiar with a new environment and learn that there are other caring adults who will look out for them. They will experience meals in a different setting and sleep in a new bed. They will wake up in the morning and know that the world is a safe place for them. Trust is being built in their friends, their friends' parents and other caring adults.

You can also talk about exciting opportunities that children experience at camp. It may be beneficial for highly anxious children (and parents) to visit local campsites beforehand. This pre-emptive approach has its benefits and limitations. Children need to cope with the unexpected, especially as they get older. Going on a school camp will bring new, exciting, unknown adventures. Experiencing these adventures with their classmates is a great bonding experience, especially if it is new for all of them. Most children will have a degree of nerves, and that is perfectly normal.

> *In order to succeed we must first believe we can.*
>
> Michael Korda

A child who displayed some anxiety in new situations had emphatically told his parents that he was not attending camp. The parents met the teacher and explained their child's anxiety. The teacher spoke with the child and his parents to explain the activities, menu and sleeping arrangements. The child remained adamant that he was not attending camp! So the parents and teacher moved on to Plan B: invoke the influence of his peers. The teacher continued talking about the upcoming camp during class. The children had to nominate cabin

buddies on the assumption that everyone was going. After auditing the cabin groups, the teacher confidentially asked some of the confident students to discuss camp with the reluctant participant in a positive light. As camp loomed large on the horizon, the boy's parents calmly prepared his clothes and materials. A couple of nights before camp, the boy began talking about what his mates had promoted. He went and had a great time, still said he wasn't going on camp the next year, and did anyway!

LESSONS LEARNED

Parents Please:

Establish routines before and after school

Embrace the diversity of the children in your child's class

Be cautious in labelling inappropriate behaviour as bullying

Teachers Please:

Establish routines at school

Meet the needs of all learners to the best of your ability

8 Learning at Home

School is only one place of learning in a child's life. Their education continues at home, in the park, at school, in private music lessons and on the sporting field. Parents need to embrace all learning opportunities, especially the informal experiences when children ask questions. In our current world, learning from home is often a formal business of remote schooling for brief or extended periods. Parents and teachers are called upon to work more closely together, and many parents are appreciating the challenges that teachers face daily at school. Teachers need to accept the limitations that parents face while educating their children at home. Together, parents and teachers can make it work.

Alternative Educational Provisions

During these unprecedented times when we are likely to engage with alternative education provisions, the need for teachers and parents to work together is more apparent than ever. We must trust each other, collaborate and ask relevant questions. Let me address a few topics relevant to remote education.

Firstly, we need to watch our use of language. We will continue to see media reports and communications on COVID-19 from health and education authorities. These frequently use emotive language when talking about the pandemic. If we minimise our use of emotive language, we can reduce its impact on our lives. It is still important to understand the seriousness of the situation in which we are living. COVID-19 needs to be managed responsibly. We must practise behaviours and habits that keep us safe and healthy. The language that we use when talking to children should tell them that although this situation is unfamiliar, it does not have to be unduly stressful. Neutral, realistic phrasing is ideal: we can talk about new experiences and new ways of doing things. We don't need to use words like 'stressful' or 'worrying'.

The flexibility that the pandemic requires of us will lead to some positive outcomes. We may end up with teachers who are increasingly skilled at delivering curriculum in alternate ways. We may find new methods of communicating effectively. Schools may have the opportunity to attend to matters that always get put on the backburner. Let's predict that education provision at home will continue on and off for the near future, with parents playing an active role in their children's learning. So, Mums and Dads: how can we make you feel confident if you're not teachers?

Ideas for Learning at Home

Establishing a timetable is a good place to start. Children want to know what to expect when they get up in the morning. They should go through the usual morning routine before starting their formal learning. If possible, learning should take place in a dedicated space.

Most children appreciate knowing the direction of each day. Create a timetable with pictures or words so that your child can track and monitor what needs to be done. Once a task is completed, tick it off. This will give you and your child a sense of achievement. Let's be realistic about the length of time during which your child will remain engaged. Children in primary school should aim to sustain their concentration for two to three hours at a time.

It is important that parents and carers understand the platforms used by their children's teachers to deliver curriculum and provide feedback. Some schools may have their own e-learning platforms. Other schools will use platforms such as Seesaw, Microsoft Teams or OneNote.

Adults and children need to have physical and mental breaks during the day. Switch off from the activity, get up, walk around, stretch your legs and go outside. Once learning activities are completed, you need to provide feedback to your child or send it to the teachers. Don't feel obliged to do this instantaneously. We all need to be kind to each other so that we can continue the business of learning while looking after our mental and physical wellbeing.

While we're working from home, we should maintain social contact as best we can with the use of technology. Allow your child access to their friends via videoconferencing, chat or telephone. Parents also need to maintain regular contact with their own networks. Whatever difficulties you are facing may be shared by other families in your community.

Other Learning Opportunities

You may have not realised the valuable learning opportunities available to you at home. Give your child the time to read and do some form of writing every day. The reading material doesn't really matter so long as it is age-appropriate. Encourage your child to respond to what they have read in writing or, if more age-appropriate, with a drawing. They may like to keep a diary. You can listen to them read aloud and give feedback on their writing, spelling and grammar. It is very important that children maintain their English literacy while learning at home.

Cooking is another fantastic learning opportunity. There is a great deal of maths involved: children will engage with measurement, counting, estimation and geometry (shapes). Cooking also

involves a variety of gross and fine motor skills. Although it might be a challenge to have a 7- or 8-year-old helping in the kitchen, please embrace the opportunity. It may also encourage children to have a healthy lifestyle (and give them an appreciation of what Mums and Dads do to prepare meals).

When children want to get outside to explore the garden, there are numerous opportunities that nature can provide for science learning. Track the growth of a plant, explore insects. Engaging with nature gives children a good physical and mental break. If they're asking questions, that's fantastic. If you don't know the answer, you now have the opportunity to research.

You may be somewhat fearful or cautious about the amount of time your child is spending online. You should limit screen time, as you do every week. There is no doubt that technology provides opportunities for learning, and you can still let your child have fun on screens.

Monitor your levels of calm. When those levels deteriorate, I encourage you to share the workload around. If children have two parents at home, both parents need to share responsibility. Single parents need to network with others so that they have a break for themselves. Even if you are adopting the role of pseudo-teacher, you are still your child's parent and teachers are still providing the curriculum.

Whether at home or at school, three conditions are necessary for children to learn. Parents and teachers need to ensure that the following conditions are universally available.

Safety

Children must feel safe. This means that they have enough food, clothing and shelter for them to concentrate on the task of learning. In some circumstances, it is necessary for the school to take on the responsibility of providing food. Breakfast clubs, which are quite common in Australia, provide children with the sustenance they need to concentrate in class. Schools also occasionally provide second-hand or even brand-new uniforms to children in need. Uniforms help children feel that they belong by minimising differences in appearance. Shelter can be provided by parents, grandparents, other relatives, foster carers or family friends. Sleeping in a warm bed is important. The other element of safety is that children know and understand their routines in life. They know who will be dropping them off at school. They know who will be picking them up. They have the confidence to walk out of the school gate at the end of the day knowing that someone who loves them will be there waiting for them.

Connectedness

A child needs to be connected to their social networks and extended family. Connection begins in the womb, then through the toddler years to school and extracurricular groups. Initially the child will be connected to family members. At school, children will ideally find others of similar interests with whom they make a connection and form part of a group. Being part of a group is key to a child's wellbeing because humans are social beings.

Contentment

Why contentment and not happiness? Happiness is an elevated state of joy that not everyone will reach. We can, however, attain contentment. My definition of contentment is the acceptance of one's circumstances. A child needs to accept their place in life: the family in which they live, the school that they attend, the social group of which they are a part, the limitations of their personal lives. They need to accept (and embrace) the opportunities that life presents them. A child who is accepting will have a degree of tolerance and understanding. This allows them to focus on the task of learning. Children who are content have a degree of comfort in themselves and their social network. Knowing that they are safe and connected allows them to explore other opportunities. Striving to improve and excel should be a goal for all lifelong learners.

The three conditions that have just been described are inextricably linked. Safety begets connection. Connection begets contentment. Contentment begets safety.

LESSONS LEARNED

Parents Please:

Engage with formal and informal learning at home

Be present with your child

Provide opportunities for fun and social connection

Teachers Please:

Provide realistic expectations for students at home

Offer support and understanding to parents

Connect with your students frequently

9 Technology

The use of technology has great merit, but also comes with risk. There is a time and place for children to use technology at home and at school. Some children have been exposed to devices and screens of various sizes from a young age. Parents may believe they are doing their children a great service by providing them with the opportunity to learn on devices before school. This may not always be the case. Using devices comes with great responsibility for parents, teachers and children. Technology is also a common vehicle of communication between parents and teachers. This is an opportunity to build trust and cooperation.

In recent years there have been many press reports about the patterns of behaviour facing children and parents living in a digital world.

There is no doubt that personal tech devices are becoming increasingly common in the lives of children. Parents are granting children permission to access social media at lower ages. Some children in primary school have their own mobile phone. Why? Parents may provide a mobile as a kind of insurance policy, so they can contact their children in the event of an emergency. This rationale makes perfect sense when the mobile phone is used just as a mobile phone. When it is used by primary school children to access social media, then we need to question the need.

Children and Social Media

As internet safety expert Brett Lee observes, the internet is an exciting and wonderful place but can be fraught with danger (Lee, 2017). Any use of the internet by children must be closely monitored by caring, responsible adults. According to Australian eSafety Commissioner Julie Inman Grant, the fact that 19 per cent of Australian teenagers  have been victims of cyberbullying indicates that this issue should be on the school curriculum (McCauley, 2018).

Why would a primary school principal be concerned that children are using social media, when the supervision of such usage would normally be the domain of parents? It is often the school staff who are called upon to deal with the fallout of online social interactions. This highlights the need for parents and schools to agree on a set of guidelines with which children are expected to comply (see Appendices 2 and 3).

When children engage in social networking, it may simply involve friendly chatter. Sadly, interactions can turn nasty or hurtful. On such occasions, distressed children often confide in parents or school staff. If parents are the first port of call, they often seek the counsel of school staff. Schools thus have an interest in managing children's usage of social media.

Popular social media apps include Instagram, Snapchat, TikTok and Facebook. The guidelines and protocols for these apps suggest that they should only be used by children 13 years of age or older. There is absolutely no need for a child in primary school to access online social networking. Children benefit from direct communication, which is most effective when understanding the 7 / 38 / 55 rule: seven per cent of communication happens through words; 38 per cent through intonation, vocal variation, volume, tone, pace and pausing; and 55 per cent through non-verbal signals (Advaney, 2017). When young people communicate via social media, they only access one aspect of communication. Children need to be more skilled in communicating before they limit themselves to a minor component. Words can be so damaging and easily misinterpreted.

Social media should be left to teenagers and adults (who still need to use it cautiously!). Let me share with you a story about why we need to protect young people from its pitfalls.

The parents of a group of 12-year-olds alerted their principal to some nasty social media exchanges. The principal asked himself if it was the school's responsibility to supervise students' access to and use of social media outside of school hours. Because the exchanges were hurtful and threatened self-esteem and wellbeing, he determined that the school had a duty of care. He talked to the student cohort and wrote to remind parents of their responsibilities. Parents reached out to express gratitude that the school had addressed the issue and made an effort to keep the children safe.

If parents endorse their children's access to social media and create accounts for them, they must accept the responsibilities of closely supervising their child's usage. Sadly, children have often been known to break agreements with their parents and their school.

It has been reported that cyberbullies have pushed young children to suicide (Squires, 2020). Age restrictions on social media apps have not prevented the traumatisation of young children. Parents should think very carefully before supporting their child's online social networking access.

I implore you to not succumb to pressure from your children, their friends or their friends' parents. Ideally, your children will be socialising with children from likeminded families and you won't have any concerns about exchanges on social media.

One of my son's friends asked him to get an Instagram account at about the age of 12. Despite pleading that all his friends had an account, our son was told that we would decline the request until he was a teenager. His friend asked if he could speak to my wife on the phone—perhaps he could persuade her directly! He dutifully asked my wife if our son could have an Instagram account. The same answer was forthcoming: 'Not just yet, but thanks for asking'. We had to make a decision in our son's best interests despite the peer pressure from his mate. As you may well appreciate, we were not popular with either boy for a brief period. We knew it was necessary to stand up and explain acceptable internet usage in our home. Parents are often reluctant to play our role and set boundaries. Remember: these boundaries keep our children safe.

I encourage parents to consider implementing the following family rules and structures when giving children access to the internet and social media:
1. Know which apps your children are accessing
2. Know the passwords and codes that allow access to these apps
3. Ensure that computers and mobile devices are used openly so that children can't hide what they're accessing
4. Keep screens out of bedrooms at night to help children's sleep and study habits, and to restrict access

Parents should know what is on their children's devices. All internet usage needs to be prudent and closely monitored. Children should be very careful when taking and storing photos or videos on their phones. They should be very careful about what they share on social media. When it comes to the internet, children have no right to privacy. We, teachers and parents, are there to protect their welfare.

Recommended School Communication Protocols

The internet and mobile phones are now central to communication between parents and schools. Because of time constraints and the volume of contacts required, school communications often rely on portals. Parents often communicate with their children's teachers via email and phone. Remember to notify the school if your email address or mobile number changes! It is recommended that parents and school staff follow some basic protocols around email and internet communication:
- Teachers respond to parent emails within 48 hours
- Parents post only positive or enquiring comments to schools on social media

It is critical that parents respect the school and its protocols. Negative or derogatory comments about the school and its staff may breach school codes of conduct for parents and volunteers (see Appendix 1). Complaints and concerns must always be communicated directly and confidentially to the school.

Email and Mobile Phones

I encourage parents to draft and reflect on emails before sending to school staff, particularly if the message is not positive. Ask a trusted friend to check the email to ensure that you are not breaking any protocols. Imagine what you would say to the teacher face-to-face. Similarly, hesitate if you have been drinking while socialising—judgement can be impaired under these circumstances! Email is recommended for explanatory messages in anticipation of or following up on a phone call.

Mobile phone communication between parents and school staff is increasingly common. While it is expected that teachers will use their work email, the decision to share their mobile number remains at their discretion. Although the efficiency of a call or text can quickly clarify a matter, parents should remember that teachers may not always have phone access during school hours.

School Social Media

Schools are becoming more adept at using social networking sites for mass communication. Many have multiple Facebook accounts, with parent groups managing their relevant sites. These sites are often accessible only by invitation. My school has established a 'Ready, Set, Prep' group as a network for parents who have children preparing for Prep.

Parents and school staff should not associate on social media. This crosses a boundary and moves the relationship from professional to personal. We are all an example to children. If any of us uses the internet for inappropriate actions, we create an example that may be followed.

Let us be respectful and safe when using the internet.

LESSONS LEARNED

Parents Please:

Monitor children's internet use

Keep your contact details up-to-date

Only publish praise about school and staff

Model good use of technology

Teachers Please:

Monitor students' use of the internet

Listen and respond to parent and child concerns

Avoid socialising with students and parents on your personal social media

Know and demonstrate the school's policies regarding internet usage and codes of conduct

Step Up and Be a Parent

Parents need to be parents to our children, and not try to be their friends. No parent wants to hurt their child, yet by default we will make decisions that they do not like. That's OK. It is important for children to understand that they will not get everything they want. Parents need to confidently take charge, make tough decisions, accept the tears and be brave enough to do what they believe is right for their child. This chapter will unpack ways to do that.

Children need parents as parents, and friends their own age. A foundation of confident parenting becomes especially important when children reach their teenage years. (While this is not the purpose of the book, I offer a word of caution based on the personal experience I am living through with a teenage son and daughter!) Parents and teachers must remember that the brains of young people are evolving. As such, conflict with them is very normal.

Parents have often spoken to me about not wanting to overstep their child's right to privacy. Let me share with you a message:

children in primary school shouldn't have any privacy. There is nothing that a child should be able to say or do or look at with which their parents are unfamiliar. Sure, it's different when children are getting dressed for swimming or having a shower. But when it comes to their computer access, their television viewing, their reading material, their friends, what they wear or what they do when they go out, children do not need any privacy. None. And if you think children have privacy rights under the age of twelve, ask yourself who will be running the household as a teenager!

Our children won't like us all the time. They won't want to hear us decline their requests. When we say no, they will be disgruntled. What would happen if we said yes to every request? Our children would not learn to cope with failure and disappointment. This is why consistent boundaries are so important. When your children learn the limitations that you have set for them, you will not find yourself having to refuse requests as often. Saying no also adds value to the times that we say yes.

When we do say no, we must follow through with it. If you don't provide a consequence for your child's behaviour, you will worsen the problem. Children pick up on our reluctance to follow through and continue to push the boundaries. Consequences need to be realistic: threatening to punish a child for a month for a minor indiscretion is not sustainable or realistic. The child will know you are bluffing. In colloquial terms, the punishment must fit the crime. Equally important is following through if we say yes to children. If we do commit to something (taking children somewhere, giving them a treat or a reward for something worthy) then let's provide it. An affirmation as promised should be very positive. If we do not follow through with affirmations or positive consequences, then we have failed our children. We must try to be consistent.

When you give children praise, do it publicly. Most children appreciate public acknowledgement from caring parents. Opportunities for praise at home might be around the dinner table, or at a family event when recognition is warranted and sincere. Opportunities at school include assemblies and praise in front of classmates. A word of caution: make sure all children get praise and recognition.

" Never stop doing your best just because someone doesn't give you credit. "

Unknown

When we were growing up, my siblings and I were not lavished with praise. Our parents are of the generation that didn't publicly praise children, yet we knew we were loved. Whenever we were introduced to our father's friends, they would congratulate us on our successes and exploits. We had no doubt that our parents were proud of us. Today's generation of parents, of which I am one, needs to be careful not to go to the opposite extreme. Give legitimate praise when warranted. If your child doesn't like being the centre of attention, be very selective about how and when you praise them.

Reprimanding and critiquing are best done privately. This prevents the child from feeling publicly embarrassed, humiliated or belittled. Respectful and sensitive correction lets children know that they are still loved but that their behaviour warrants some criticism.

We are role models for our children. Our attitude and response to rules will be mimicked. If parents follow school protocols and reinforce expectations, children will (or should) follow their example. If parents struggle with school protocols and expectations, they are encouraged to discuss their concerns with the relevant school staff.

One of the other great challenges of being a parent is allowing children to make some of their own decisions at an appropriate age and regarding appropriate topics. For example, a child doesn't get to choose which uniform to wear to school. Children also don't necessarily choose the food they eat. They should be provided with healthy—and ideally varied—meals, but should not dictate what, when or how they will eat. These are basic courtesies that they will learn to adopt in recognising the differences between their parents' and their own roles in life.

I know a mother who makes a different meal for her 10-year-old son most nights because he doesn't like what the rest of the family eats. In a word, that is silly. The mother is making a rod for her back by letting her child dictate what he eats. She is providing a poor diet for the child and overreacting to very ordinary behaviour. She should  *provide the same meal for all her family; if her son chooses something else then he either makes his own meal or goes hungry (which won't last long). Either way, he will learn to eat family meals or be independent in cooking for himself. Win win.*

Parents often choose schools to be with likeminded people. In today's world, there are numerous models of families and parenting. Primary school parents can range anywhere from teenagers to people in their 60s. Older parents may have started having children later in life; they could be in their second or third relationship; they could be foster parents; they could have children spread out over many years. I have enrolled children from many family models, including parents who were already grandparents. There may be single parents by virtue of separation, divorce, widowhood or choice. There may be same-sex couples.

The one thing all these families have in common is that they have children requiring an education. They will hopefully be united in valuing education and the philosophy that the school promotes. Each family is responsible for building a relationship with school staff and vice versa. This is done through communication.

As with all relationships, that between home and school may not run a smooth road all the time. There can be conflicts between students and teachers or teachers and parents. Such occasions require mutual resolutions.

Conflict

When children are involved in school conflicts or acts of non-compliance, parents must help them learn negotiation skills to comply with expectations. Once a parent becomes aware of a conflict involving their child, their response will send a message to the child and the teachers. If a parent makes an excuse for a child's poor behaviour, this means they can rationalise a poor decision their child has made. If a parent gives an explanation or reason for a child's behaviour, they are providing a legitimate story to explain why something doesn't comply. Let me give you some examples:

Scenario 1: Child doesn't wear correct uniform to school

Parents' excuse: Child said that her peers don't wear the uniform, so why should she?

Parents' excuse: It is her final year of primary school, so no need to worry about the expense of school shoes when she has secondary school next year with more expenses.

Parents' reason: Shoes are too small after growth spurt and we will have the correct uniform within the next week.

Scenario 2: Child has had an argument with a peer at school and the other child's parents have complained to the school

Parents' excuse: The other child started the conflict, and my child was just defending himself.
Parents' excuse: My child is struggling with friends and was just trying to fit in.

Parents' reason: My child needs to learn better resolution skills as he is immature, and we will work with the school to train and upskill him.

The parents who made excuses sided with the child, not the school. They rationalised their child's poor choices and behaviours. The parents who gave an explanation acknowledged the behaviour and agreed to follow school protocols as soon as possible. They are supporting the school to build a culture of trust, collaboration and enquiry.

Behaviour

Some children are naturally responsible, others not so much. The two types can be found in the same family! This is a classic reminder of the nature-versus-nurture debate. Here's the good news: whatever challenges you are experiencing, you can almost guarantee that other parents and teachers have been through similar! We cannot expect perfection from our children in anything. We can expect improvement—not linear, but more like climbing a mountain. There will be ups and downs, and this is perfectly normal.

Children are still like babies in some ways: crankiness often stems from fatigue or hunger. (This of course gets more complicated with school and social demands.) When checking on children, start with the basics. If a child is not performing as expected or is out of character, look to food and fatigue before you examine friendships and relationships. It is important to feed children when cranky: they are much calmer to talk to when fed and watered!

It is common for teachers and parents to see different personalities in the same child. What do I mean? A child who can be a perfect angel at school may be challenging at home. Teachers are very grateful that they usually see the good side of a child's personality. Occasionally, disbelieving parents will discover that their angel misbehaves at school. These parents tend to be the lawnmower types who keep everything smooth for their children. Not healthy for child or parent.

Children need to own their mistakes. Parents also need to own their children's mistakes. If the school contacts you about your child's behaviour, it is important to listen before judging. Remember those three questions from Chapter 4 and choose the right one to ask ('please tell me what happened'). I also suggest that parents believe school staff. Children have the tendency to embellish or be selective about details of stories, so we need to be cautious about taking a child's version of events as the gospel truth. Hopefully our children will learn from their mistakes and the feedback they receive. Lessons learnt build resilience in children.

> *I am blessed to make so many mistakes in my life, so I can learn from them.*
>
> *Michael Grinder*

Freedom

As caring adults, we need to let our children fall down and get back up again. This is meant both figuratively and literally. Bumps and bruises, scrapes and skinned knees are all part of growing up. It is of course important that parents and teachers create and maintain a safe environment in which children will grow and learn. The amount of freedom allowed to children has lessened since I was a boy. Children of forty years ago could jump on their bicycles, meet friends and disappear for hours riding and exploring the neighbourhood—all without a mobile phone. Times have changed and we need to be diligent in monitoring our children's whereabouts and activities.

Healthy communication with caring adults is vital for children to grow into confident contributors to society. Accepting that every child's personality is different, we should sensitively respond to children and initiate communication. Parents and teachers must have patience.

Let your child talk when they arrive home from school. Don't bombard them with questions as soon as you pick them up. Stereotypes often hold true: Dads want to solve problems and Mums want to keep their 'babies'. One of the hardest things for parents to do is listen and allow silent space. Eventually, children will speak and fill that space.

Families often catch up on the events of their day around the dinner table. Eating meals together is important when possible (accepting the busy nature of our lives these days). When asking about school, it is most productive to pose specific questions about activities or subjects. Children often respond to general questions with one- or two-word answers. Some helpful questions might be:
- Who did you play with today? What did you do?
- What did you learn about in that subject?
- What's happening at school tomorrow?

If your child's behaviour is challenging, remember that every day is a new day. Ask the questions above. Please don't ask your child if they got into trouble. This becomes a self-fulfilling prophecy because you show your child that you expect them to be naughty at school.

We often find it difficult to take the time to talk and listen to children. When can we do it? Talking in the car to and from school is a great opportunity. This is a brief period of no escape when the child can be the centre of attention! Another great time and place is at night when children are going to bed. As not all children want to be seen when they are sharing personal stories, darkness may allow them to reveal their concerns of the day. As adults, we must learn to listen (as my children often say, 'You don't understand!' to which I respond, 'I'm trying!'). One of the hardest things is not to fill in the gaps of silence, especially when you ask sons a question and they take time to answer. Daughters are more likely to chat; sons may not. Allow them time to answer. My children often call me to their room at night to chat. Darkness is a great leveller.

Once you have your child talking, please read their verbal and non-verbal cues. What may seem insignificant to you may mean the world to them. Don't trivialise their problem because you don't think it's a big deal. What to us as adults may seem 'funny' may be important to them. Not everything is a joke—just use humour (not sarcasm!) as a release valve at times if appropriate.

If your child is distressed and seeking inappropriate attention at the wrong time, it may be necessary to distract them by changing topics. If your child is being 'silly' about something, change topics. This takes a subtle skill from parents and teachers. You can acknowledge their topic and assure them that you will get back to their concern at the appropriate time.

> *Matthew was concerned that one of his sons was cranky with him when they were discussing his schoolwork. Eventually his son gave him the message: 'You only tell me the bad news, Dad.' This was a wake-up call for Matthew, who became more conscious about balancing his feedback to his son. Matthew was also pleased that his son's school had alerted him that his son was out of sorts.*

As children grow up, there will be inevitable mood swings. If they have the basics of sleep, food, relaxation and exercise then their minds and bodies will work better. When problems do arise, it is important for parents to listen and correct constructively.

LESSONS LEARNED

Parents Please:

Don't be afraid to say no

Follow school protocols and give reasons instead of excuses

Ask your children specific questions

Teachers Please:

Follow through and be consistent with consequences for bad behaviour

Take the time to listen

Be patient with parents when delivering bad news

Conclusion

This isn't the final word.

Education will continue to evolve and so must the relationship between parents and teachers. Schools play a central role in fixing and preventing societal issues. Together, we can have a positive impact on the lives of the children under our care.

Education is complicated, but we can't be frightened by its complexity. Many things that will affect a child's achievement happen in the classroom. Let's embrace this challenge and work together to grow opportunities for children to achieve at school and at home.

Our brains become fatigued when we overanalyse what should be simple decisions. All humans make hundreds of decisions every day. Some people make quick decisions and live with the consequences. Others may procrastinate and struggle to make any decisions. Some make measured decisions after reflecting on possible and probable outcomes. We need to be both thoughtful and confident when working with children. In this way, we can individually and collectively make wise decisions to their benefit.

As a young adult I enjoyed playing grade cricket in Brisbane. During a pre-season training session, my wise elderly coach saw that I was struggling to bat to my greatest ability. He had a quiet word with me and told me this: too much analysis causes paralysis. I have often used that phrase when encouraging people to make decisions. We need to be wise, prudent and reflective—but also decisive.

There is a definite sharing of responsibilities in children's education. Parents are the first educators of their children. To be ready for school, children need skills that will allow them to engage with the learning process. Parents must learn how to build relationships with teachers and other parents. How we go about building these relationships in a culture of trust, collaboration and enquiry is key to our children's successful educational journey.

Parents and teachers hold multifaceted responsibilities to children. As the first educators, parents mould their children in the safe confines of the home. As soon as a child goes to school, they will be mixing with peers whose parents have different values and beliefs. How parents navigate these relationships is important. There are also the transitions and new experiences that every child faces at home and at school. How parents manage these experiences may influence their child's wellbeing and relationships at school.

Communication is one of the most important skills that adults need to work in harmony. As our newest Olympian decathlete Ash Moloney will attest, people can achieve great things when they work together. Ash received the bronze medal at the 2021 Tokyo Olympics after being spurred on by his fellow Aussie decathlete Cedric Dubler. Although out of medal contention himself, Cedric ran alongside his mate encouraging him to work hard and achieve success. We need to heed that model of collaboration.

As our world evolves, so do opportunities for children. The use of technology grows exponentially. Learning within the home has changed for a variety of reasons. Family models have changed. Each of these things affects a child's ability to be ready for school and learning. How parents and teachers navigate these environments will strongly influence children's healthy development.

    Parents and teachers must trust our instincts. We can sleep easy knowing that we have the tools to act in the best interests of our children.

Bibliography

Acceptable Use of Computer and Internet Resources (2016). Our Lady of the Rosary School, Kenmore.
Acceptable Use of Technology and Internet Resources Consent Form (2016). Our Lady of the Rosary School, Kenmore.
Advaney, M. (2017). To Talk or Not to Talk That Is the Question! *Youth Time Magazine*. https://youth-time.eu/to-talk-or-not-to-talk-that-is-the-question-at-least-70-percent-of-communication-is-non-verbal/
Australian Bureau of Statistics (2018). *4364.0.55.001 - National Health Survey: First Results, 2017–18*. Data table 16.1. http://www.abs.gov.au/AUSSTATS/
Australian Council for Educational Research (2012). *National School Improvement Tool*. https://www.acer.org/au/school-improvement/improvement-tools/national-school-improvement-tool/
Biddulph, S. (2019). *Raising Boys in the Twenty-First Century*. Sydney: Simon & Schuster.
Biddulph, S. (2019). *Raising Girls in the Twenty-First Century*. Sydney: Simon & Schuster.

Brisbane Catholic Education Office (2020). *Code of Conduct for Volunteers and Other Personnel.* Catholic Education Archdiocese of Brisbane. https://www.bne.catholic.edu.au/students-parents/student-protection/Documents/COC-Volunteers-Other-Personnel.pdf/

Cameron, W. B. (1963). *Informal Sociology, a casual introduction to sociological thinking.* New York: Random House.

Carmody, R. (2018). How to tell if you have a gifted and talented child, and what to do about it. *ABC News.* https://www.abc.net.au/news/2018-10-22/how-to-tell-if-you-have-a-gifted-child-explainer/10393244/

Carr-Gregg, M. & Robinson, E. (2017). *The Prince Boofhead Syndrome: Surviving Adolescent Boys.* Sydney: Penguin.

Carr-Gregg, M. & Robinson, E. (2017). *The Princess Bitchface Syndrome 2.0: Surviving Adolescent Girls.* Sydney: Penguin.

Dweck, C. (2017). *Mindset: Changing the Way You Think to Fulfil Your Potential.* London: Robinson.

Fuller, A. (2015). *Unlocking Your Child's Genius: How to Discover and Encourage Your Child's Natural Talents.* Melbourne: Finch Publishing.

Gleeson, C. (2018). *A Canopy of Stars: Some Reflections for the Journey.* Melbourne: David Lovell Publishing.

Grinder, M. (2006). *ENVoY Educational Non-Verbal Yardsticks: Your Personal Guide to Classroom Management.* Self-published. 7th edition.

Hattie, J. (2009). *Visible Learning: A Synthesis of Over 800 Meta-Analyses Relating to Achievement.* Oxon: Routledge.

Henderson, A. & Berla, N. (1994). *A New Generation of Evidence: The Family Is Critical to Student Achievement.* Columbia, MD: National Committee for Citizens in Education.

Honoré, C. (2010). *In Praise of Slow: How a Worldwide Movement Is Challenging the Cult of Speed.* London: Orion Publishing.

Honoré, C. (2009). *Under Pressure: Rescuing Our Children from the Culture of Hyper-Parenting.* London: Orion Publishing.

Korda, M. (1977). *Success!* New York: Random House.

Lavoie, R. (unknown). *Fairness: To Each According to His Needs.* https://www.ricklavoie.com/fairnessart.html

Lee, B. (2017). *Screen Resolution: Keeping Children Safe Online*. North Richmond, NSW: Aurora House.

Lillico, I. (2004). *Homework and the Homework Grid*. Self-published.

Locke, J. (2015). *The Bonsai Child: Why modern parenting limits children's potential and practical strategies to turn it around*. Self-published.

Maslow, A. (1943). A theory of human motivation. *Psychological Review*, 50(4), 370–396. https://doi.org/10.1037/h0054346

McCauley, D. (2018, 3 October). Cyber bullying needs to be on school curriculum, says eSafety Commissioner. *The Sydney Morning Herald*.

Molloy, S. (2014, 10 December). The Project forced to apologise over Santa Claus comments by Kitty Flanagan. *Perth Now*. https://www.perthnow.com.au/entertainment/tv/the-project-forced-to-apologise-over-santa-claus-comments-by-kitty-flanagan-ng-f37707e8ba31b96077b49629fa3e75c0

Parent / Volunteer Code of Conduct (2016). Our Lady of the Rosary School, Kenmore.

Parker, A. (2019). *The Negotiator's Toolkit*. Potts Point, NSW: Peak Performance Development.

Richardson, N. (2018). Stories Make Us: In Conversation with Morris Gleitzman. *Connections*, Issue 105, Term 2, ISSN 2207-8924.

Rock, D. (2017). *Your Brain at Work: Strategies for Overcoming Distraction, Regaining Focus, and Working Smarter All Day Long*. New York: Harpers Business.

Salisbury, C. (2011). Rod Welford Interviewed by Chris Salisbury. *Queensland Speaks*. https://www.queenslandspeaks.com.au/rod-welford/

Speech Sounds Development Chart (2021). Kid Sense. https://childdevelopment.com.au/resources/child-development-charts/speech-sounds-developmental-chart/

Squires, A. (2020). Social Media, Self-Esteem, and Teen Suicide. *PCC Pediatric EHR Solutions*. https://blog.pcc.com/social-media-self-esteem-and-teen-suicide/

Volunteers Code of Conduct (2015). Brisbane Catholic Education, Archdiocese of Brisbane.

Vonow, B. (2017, 24 August). 'Always kiss them goodnight': Grieving dad's heartbreaking '10 lessons learned' since son died aged just 3 from sudden brain bleed. *The Sun.* https://www.thesun.co.uk/news/4312700/grieving-dad-10-lessons-learned-since-son-died/

Appendices

Appendix 1: Parent / Volunteer Code of Conduct (extract)
Provided with the permission of Our Lady of the Rosary School, Kenmore

Parents / Volunteers should treat students and staff with respect:
- Treat everyone with courtesy, sensitivity, tact, consideration and humility.
- Respect the cultures, beliefs, opinions and decisions of others although you not always agree.

Parent / Volunteer responsibilities:
- Value and champion your school and its reputation. Be mindful of the hurt and damage social media may cause to staff members and other parents.
- Respect the rights of staff members and other individuals.

As a Parent / Volunteer we ask that you:
- Understand the importance of a healthy parent / teacher / child relationship and communicate any concerns to your school in a constructive and appropriate manner.
- Maintain a positive and cooperative attitude and interact positively with other parents and members of the school community.

Appendix 2: Acceptable Use of Technology and Internet Resources Consent Form

Provided with the permission of Our Lady of the Rosary School, Kenmore

Acceptable Use of Technology and Internet Resources Consent Form

This Consent Form must be signed and returned prior to students being granted access to the Internet and other information and communication technology resources.

Parents / guardians are encouraged to review and discuss the contents of the Acceptable Use of Computer and Internet Resources policy with the student and answer any questions that they may have. Any queries in relation to this material should be directed to **the school principal.**

By signing this Consent Form, both parents / guardians and students are agreeing to the terms of access as set out in the Acceptable Use of Computer and Internet Resources policy and acknowledge that they will be responsible in the event of any breach and that appropriate disciplinary steps may result.

Student Acceptance

I agree to comply with all requirements as set out in the Acceptable Use of Computer and Internet Resources policy and all other relevant laws and restrictions in my access to the various information and communication technology resources through the Brisbane Catholic Education and school network.

NAME: _____ PC CLASS: _____

SIGNATURE: _____ DATE: _____

Parent / Guardian Consent

As the parent or legal guardian of the student named above, I grant permission for the student named above to access the various information and communication technology resources (including email and the Internet).

I understand that access is granted to students subject to the restrictions contained in the Acceptable Use of Computers and Internet Resources policy and that if breached, consequences may follow.

I acknowledge that some material available on the Internet may be objectionable and that in addition to the Acceptable Use of Computer and Internet Resources statement, I have discussed appropriate restrictions for the student when accessing or sharing information or material over the Internet.

NAME: _____   DATE: _____

SIGNATURE: _____

Appendix 3: Acceptable Use of Computer and Internet Resources

Provided with the permission of Our Lady of the Rosary School, Kenmore

Acceptable Use of Computer and Internet Resources Extract

Computer and Internet resources have become of critical importance to schools in facilitating and supporting learning and teaching. **Technology resources are provided to students for educational purposes only.**

[College Name] have established significant computing and communication resources to support these activities.

This document has been developed to inform users of their rights, responsibilities and obligations when using Computer and Internet resources, consistent with Brisbane Catholic Education's requirements that all such resources are used in an ethical, legal and responsible manner.

The requirements and rules set out below apply to all **[College Name]** technology resources whether they are accessed through computers owned by the school or through privately owned devices (for example, accessing school Internet through a personal notebook or telephone).

Responsibilities of Users

Students must comply with the rules for accessing technology resources in this document.

Permitted Use of Technology Resources

Students must only access **[College Name]** technology resources for school work.

Students must not:
- buy or sell items or services over the Internet;
- access or enter chat rooms;
- access, post or send inappropriate internet or email content, especially content that is illegal, dangerous, obscene or offensive;
- amend documents created by another student without that student's consent;
- download, install or use unauthorised computer programs;
- deliberately install computer viruses or other malicious programs;
- gain unauthorised access to any system by any means;
- use technology resources to attack or compromise another system or network;
- access or intercept emails sent to other persons.

Confidentiality and Cybersafety

Students should be aware that material that they post on Internet sites (including Facebook and other social media sites) is **public**. The content of public posts may have personal implications for students if, for example, potential employers access that material. The content of posts also reflects on our educational institution and community as a whole. Once information is on the internet it may not be possible to remove it.

Students should not display personal information about themselves or others in a way that is public. For example, students should not post their own or anyone else's address, telephone number or other personal details on the Internet or communicate these details in emails. Students should not distribute someone else's personal information without their permission.

Where disclosure of personal information is made through authorised avenues (for example, by the use of email or an official website), users should be aware that invasions of privacy may sometimes occur and it is outside **[College Name]** control to prevent such instances from occurring.

Students should be aware that persons on the Internet might not be who they say they are. Students must not arrange to meet persons who they have met on the Internet.

The operation and maintenance of technology resources often requires the backup and caching of data, the logging of activity and the monitoring of general usage patterns and as such, complete confidentiality and privacy cannot be guaranteed. **[College Name]** may also be required to inspect or provide copies of electronic communications where required to by law, or where the investigation of possible misuses of technology resources is required.

Cyberbullying and Defamation

Students must not use email or the Internet to say mean, rude or unkind things about other people or send threatening, harassing or offensive messages. Improper use of technology resources could amount to defamation.

About the Author

Andrew has been in primary school education for over 30 years. He has three main areas of professional interest, each focused on building a culture of trust, collaboration and enquiry within the community.

School Readiness: assisting parents to prepare their children to attend to learning at school by developing their independence, social skills, speech and language development, and gross and fine motor skills. As Andrew has noticed a decline in these skills over the last 10 years (supported by research), it is more important than ever that parents be prepared for their children to start school. If we want children to achieve success, then parents, teachers and early childhood educators must work together to make a positive difference in the lives of children.

Parent / Teacher Partnerships: consistent communication protocols between parents and teachers develops a culture of trust, collaboration and enquiry. When parents and teachers have the same philosophy, children are the beneficiaries of their combined efforts. Parents cannot provide a complete education without teachers. Teachers cannot provide a complete education without parents.

Mentoring and Coaching Early-Career Principals: supporting new principals as they negotiate the start of their principalship.

Watch out for Andrew's next book, *Balance: Building Positive Relationships Within Protocols*, to be published in 2022.

Contact Andrew on:
0409 872 621
andrew@oberthur.org
www.creativecollaborativesolutions.net

www.ingramcontent.com/pod-product-compliance
Lightning Source LLC
Chambersburg PA
CBHW071631080526
44588CB00010B/1358